Performance Testing with JMeter 2.9

Learn how to test web applications using Apache JMeter with practical, hands-on examples

Bayo Erinle

[PACKT] open source*
PUBLISHING   community experience distilled

BIRMINGHAM - MUMBAI

Performance Testing with JMeter 2.9

First published: July 2013

Production Reference: 1220713

Published by Packt Publishing Ltd.
Livery Place
35 Livery Street
Birmingham B3 2PB, UK.

ISBN 978-1-78216-584-2

www.packtpub.com

Cover Image by Suresh Mogre (suresh.mogre.99@gmail.com)

Credits

Author

Bayo Erinle

Reviewers

Dmitri Nevedrov

Shantonu Sarker

Acquisition Editor

Kevin Colaco

Commissioning Editor

Llewellyn F. Rozario

Technical Editors

Anita Nayak

Sampreshita Maheshwari

Copy Editors

Aditya Nair

Laxmi Subramanian

Project Coordinator

Sherin Padayatty

Proofreader

Stephen Silk

Indexer

Hemangini Bari

Graphics

Abhinash Sahu

Ronak Dhruv

Production Coordinator

Zahid Shaikh

Cover Work

Zahid Shaikh

About the Author

Bayo Erinle is a senior software engineer with over nine years' experience in designing, developing, testing, and architecting software. He has worked in various spectrums of the IT field, including government, finance, and health care. As a result, he has been involved in the planning, development, implementation, integration, and testing of numerous applications, including multi-tiered, standalone, distributed, and cloud-based applications. He is always intrigued by new technology and enjoys learning new things. He currently resides in Maryland, US, and when he is not hacking away at some new technology, he enjoys spending time with his wife Nimota and their three children, Mayowa, Durotimi, and Fisayo.

About the Reviewers

Dmitri Nevedrov has been working in software research and development for many years, primarily focusing on Java, J2EE technology, and performance optimization techniques. He lives in Denver, Colorado.

Shantonu Sarker is a proactive software test engineer with seven years of experience in test automation, development (C# and Java), and project management with Agile (Scrum and Kanban). Currently, he is working as Senior SQA (Automation Lead) at *Relisource Technologies Ltd*. He also owns a startup software company named *QualitySofts*, which specializes in software development and testing services. He also gives training on software development (C# and Java) and software test tools contractually.

He started his career as a software developer and trainer back in 2008. Before starting his career in the software industry, he was a computer teacher.

He has attended two professional training programs from BASIS (Bangladesh Association for Software and Information Services) on OOP, Industry Ready and OOAD. He has completed the *ISTQB* and *JLPT-L3 and L4* courses, and has procured the *JLPT-L4* certification (from the Japan Foundation) when he was in *BJIT Ltd*. He also completed his training on *Agile* (Kanban and Scrum) by Naresh Jain and *Software Security* by Nahidul Kibria when he was with *KAZ Software*. He completed his BSc. from *Institute of Science Trade & Technology*, which is under the *National University of Bangladesh*. His thesis subject was *Object Oriented Unit Testing*.

I would like to thank Guru Mahajatok, because without his guidance I would not be what I am today. He is a great inspiration to me.

www.PacktPub.com

Support files, eBooks, discount offers, and more

You might want to visit www.PacktPub.com for support files and downloads related to your book.

Did you know that Packt offers eBook versions of every book published, with PDF and ePub files available? You can upgrade to the eBook version at www.PacktPub.com and as a print book customer, you are entitled to a discount on the eBook copy. Get in touch with us at service@packtpub.com for more details.

At www.PacktPub.com, you can also read a collection of free technical articles, sign up for a range of free newsletters and receive exclusive discounts and offers on Packt books and eBooks.

http://PacktLib.PacktPub.com

Do you need instant solutions to your IT questions? PacktLib is Packt's online digital book library. Here, you can access, read and search across Packt's entire library of books.

Why Subscribe?

- Fully searchable across every book published by Packt
- Copy and paste, print and bookmark content
- On demand and accessible via web browser

Free Access for Packt account holders

If you have an account with Packt at www.PacktPub.com, you can use this to access PacktLib today and view nine entirely free books. Simply use your login credentials for immediate access.

Table of Contents

Preface

Performance Testing with JMeter 2.9 is about a type of testing intended to determine the responsiveness, reliability, throughput, interoperability, and scalability of a system and/or application under a given workload. It is critical and essential to the success of any software product launch and its maintenance. It also plays an integral part in scaling an application out to support a wider user base.

Apache JMeter is a free open source, cross-platform performance testing tool that has been around since the late 90s. It is mature, robust, portable, and highly extensible. It has a large user base and offers lots of plugins to aid testing.

This is a practical hands-on book that focuses on how to leverage Apache JMeter to meet your testing needs. It starts with a quick introduction on performance testing, but quickly moves into engaging topics such as recording test scripts, monitoring system resources, an extensive look at several JMeter components, leveraging the cloud for testing, and extending Apache JMeter capabilities via plugins. Along the way, you will do some scripting, learn and use tools such as Vagrant, Puppet, Apache Tomcat, and be armed with all the knowledge you need to take on your next testing engagement.

Whether you are a developer or tester, this book is sure to give you some valuable knowledge to aid you in attaining success in your future testing endeavors.

What this book covers

Chapter 1, *Performance Testing Fundamentals*, covers the fundamentals of performance testing and the installation and configuration of JMeter.

Chapter 2, *Recording Your First Test*, dives into recording your first JMeter test script and covers the anatomy of a JMeter test script.

Chapter 3, *Submitting Forms*, covers form submission in detail. It includes handling various HTML form elements, (checkboxes, radio buttons, file uploads, downloads, and so on), JSON data, and XML.

Chapter 4, *Managing Sessions*, explains session management, including cookies and URL rewriting.

Chapter 5, *Resource Monitoring*, dives into active monitoring of system resources while executing tests. You get to start up a server and extend JMeter via plugins.

Chapter 6, *Distributed Testing*, takes an in-depth look at leveraging the cloud for performance testing. We dive into tools such as Vagrant, Puppet, and AWS.

Chapter 7, *Helpful Tips*, provides you with helpful techniques and tips for getting the most out of JMeter.

What you need for this book

To follow along with the examples in this book, you will need the following:

- A computer with an Internet connection
- Apache JMeter (http://jmeter.apache.org/)
- Java Runtime Environment (JRE) or Java Development Kit (JDK) (http://www.oracle.com/technetwork/java/javase/downloads/index.html)

In addition, for *Chapter 4*, *Resource Monitoring*, you need the following:

- Apache Tomcat (http://tomcat.apache.org/download-70.cgi)

And for *Chapter 6*, *Distributed Testing*, you need the following:

- Vagrant (http://www.vagrantup.com/)
- An AWS account (http://aws.amazon.com/)

The book contains pointers and additional helpful links in setting all these up.

Who this book is for

The book is targeted primarily at developers and testers. Developers who have always been intrigued by performance testing and wanted to dive in on the action will find it extremely useful and gain insightful skills as they walk through the practical examples in the book.

Testers will also benefit from this book since it will guide them through solving practical, real-world challenges when testing modern web applications, giving them ample knowledge to aid them in becoming better testers. Additionally, they will be exposed to certain helpful testing tools that will come in handy at some point in their testing careers.

Conventions

In this book, you will find a number of styles of text that distinguish between different kinds of information. Here are some examples of these styles, and an explanation of their meaning.

Code words in text, database table names, folder names, filenames, file extensions, pathnames, dummy URLs, user input, and Twitter handles are shown as follows: "Append %JAVA_HOME%/bin to the end of the existing path value (if any)."

A block of code is set as follows:

```
DROP TABLE IF EXISTS TEST;
CREATE TABLE TEST(ID INT PRIMARY KEY, NAME VARCHAR(255));
INSERT INTO TEST VALUES(1, 'Hello');
INSERT INTO TEST VALUES(2, 'World');
```

When we wish to draw your attention to a particular part of a code block, the relevant lines or items are set in bold:

```
DROP TABLE IF EXISTS TEST;
CREATE TABLE TEST(ID INT PRIMARY KEY, NAME VARCHAR(255));
INSERT INTO TEST VALUES(1, 'Hello');
INSERT INTO TEST VALUES(2, 'World');
```

Any command-line input or output is written as follows:

```
./jmeter.sh -H proxy.server -P7567 -u username -a password
```

New terms and **important words** are shown in bold. Words that you see on the screen, in menus or dialog boxes for example, appear in the text like this: "clicking the **Next** button moves you to the next screen".

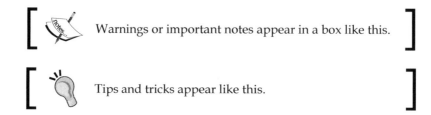

> Warnings or important notes appear in a box like this.

> Tips and tricks appear like this.

Reader feedback

Feedback from our readers is always welcome. Let us know what you think about this book — what you liked or may have disliked. Reader feedback is important for us to develop titles that you really get the most out of.

To send us general feedback, simply send an e-mail to feedback@packtpub.com, and mention the book title via the subject of your message.

If there is a topic that you have expertise in and you are interested in either writing or contributing to a book, see our author guide on www.packtpub.com/authors.

Customer support

Now that you are the proud owner of a Packt book, we have a number of things to help you to get the most from your purchase.

Downloading the example code

You can download the example code files for all Packt books you have purchased from your account at http://www.packtpub.com. If you purchased this book elsewhere, you can visit http://www.packtpub.com/support and register to have the files e-mailed directly to you.

Downloading the color images of this book

We also provide you a PDF file that has color images of the screenshots/diagrams used in this book. The color images will help you better understand the changes in the output. You can download this file from `http://www.packtpub.com/sites/default/files/downloads/5842OS_graphics.pdf`.

Errata

Although we have taken every care to ensure the accuracy of our content, mistakes do happen. If you find a mistake in one of our books—maybe a mistake in the text or the code—we would be grateful if you would report this to us. By doing so, you can save other readers from frustration and help us improve subsequent versions of this book. If you find any errata, please report them by visiting `http://www.packtpub.com/submit-errata`, selecting your book, clicking on the **errata submission form** link, and entering the details of your errata. Once your errata are verified, your submission will be accepted and the errata will be uploaded on our website, or added to any list of existing errata, under the Errata section of that title. Any existing errata can be viewed by selecting your title from `http://www.packtpub.com/support`.

Piracy

Piracy of copyright material on the Internet is an ongoing problem across all media. At Packt, we take the protection of our copyright and licenses very seriously. If you come across any illegal copies of our works, in any form, on the Internet, please provide us with the location address or website name immediately so that we can pursue a remedy.

Please contact us at `copyright@packtpub.com` with a link to the suspected pirated material.

We appreciate your help in protecting our authors, and our ability to bring you valuable content.

Questions

You can contact us at `questions@packtpub.com` if you are having a problem with any aspect of the book, and we will do our best to address it.

1

Performance Testing Fundamentals

Baysoft Training Inc. is an emerging startup company focused on redefining how software will help get more people trained in various fields in the IT industry. The company achieves this goal by providing a suite of products, including online courses, onsite training, and offsite training. As such, one of their flagship products, TrainBot—a web-based application—is focused solely on registering individuals for courses of interest that will aid them in attaining career goals. Once registered, the client can then go on to take a series of interactive online courses.

The incident

Up until recently, traffic on TrainBot had been light as it had only been opened to a handful of clients, since it was still in closed beta. Everything was fully operational and the application as a whole was very responsive. Just a few weeks ago, TrainBot was open to the public and all was still good and dandy. To celebrate the launch and promote its online training courses, Baysoft Training Inc. recently offered 75 percent off for all the training courses. However, that promotional offer caused a sudden influx on TrainBot, far beyond what the company had anticipated. Web traffic shot up by 300 percent and suddenly things took a turn for the worse. Network resources weren't holding up well, server CPUs and memory were at 90-95 percent and database servers weren't far behind due to high I/O and contention. As a result, most web requests began to get slower response times, making TrainBot totally unresponsive for most of its first-time clients. It didn't take too long after that for the servers to crash and for the support lines to get flooded.

The aftermath

It was a long night at BaySoft Training Inc. corporate office. How did this happen? Could this have been avoided? Why was the application and system not able to handle the load? Why weren't adequate performance and stress tests conducted on the system and application? Was it an application problem, a system resource issue or a combination of both? All of these were questions management demanded answers to from the group of engineers, which comprised software developers, network and system engineers, quality assurance (QA) testers, and database administrators gathered in the WAR room. There sure was a lot of finger pointing and blame to go around the room. After a little brainstorming, it wasn't too long for the group to decide what needed to be done. The application and its system resources will need to undergo extensive and rigorous testing. This will include all facets of the application and all supporting system resources, including, but not limited to, infrastructure, network, database, servers, and load balancers. Such a test will help all the involved parties to discover exactly where the bottlenecks are and address them accordingly.

Performance testing

Performance testing is a type of testing intended to determine the responsiveness, reliability, throughput, interoperability, and scalability of a system and/or application under a given workload. It could also be defined as a process of determining the speed or effectiveness of a computer, network, software application, or device. Testing can be conducted on software applications, system resources, targeted application components, databases, and a whole lot more. It normally involves an automated test suite as this allows for easy, repeatable simulations of a variety of normal, peak, and exceptional load conditions. Such forms of testing help verify whether a system or application meets the specifications claimed by its vendor. The process can compare applications in terms of parameters such as speed, data transfer rate, throughput, bandwidth, efficiency, or reliability. Performance testing can also aid as a diagnostic tool in determining bottlenecks and single points of failure. It is often conducted in a controlled environment and in conjunction with stress testing; a process of determining the ability of a system or application to maintain a certain level of effectiveness under unfavorable conditions.

Why bother? Using Baysoft's case study mentioned earlier, it should be obvious why companies bother and go through great lengths to conduct performance testing. Disaster could have been minimized, if not totally eradicated, if effective performance testing had been conducted on TrainBot prior to opening it up to the masses. As we go ahead in this chapter, we will continue to explore the many benefits of effective performance testing.

At a very high level, performance testing is always almost conducted to address one or more risks related to expense, opportunity costs, continuity, and/or corporate reputation. Conducting such tests help give insights to software application release readiness, adequacy of network and system resources, infrastructure stability, and application scalability, just to name a few. Gathering estimated performance characteristics of application and system resources prior to the launch helps to address issues early and provides valuable feedback to stakeholders, helping them make key and strategic decisions.

Performance testing covers a whole lot of ground including areas such as:

- Assessing application and system production readiness
- Evaluating against performance criteria
- Comparing performance characteristics of multiple systems or system configurations
- Identifying source of performance bottlenecks
- Aiding with performance and system tuning
- Helping to identify system throughput levels
- Testing tool

Most of these areas are intertwined with each other, each aspect contributing to attaining the overall objectives of stakeholders. However, before jumping right in, let's take a moment to understand the core activities in conducting performance tests:

- **Identify the test environment**: Becoming familiar with the physical test and production environments is crucial to a successful test run. Knowing things, such as the hardware, software, and network configurations of the environment help derive an effective test plan and identify testing challenges from the outset. In most cases, these will be revisited and/or revised during the testing cycle.

- **Identify acceptance criteria**: What is the acceptable performance of the various modules of the application under load? Specifically, identify the response time, throughput, and resource utilization goals and constraints. How long should the end user wait before rendering a particular page? How long should the user wait to perform an operation? Response time is usually a user concern, throughput a business concern, and resource utilization a system concern. As such, response time, throughput, and resource utilization are key aspects of performance testing. Acceptance criteria is usually driven by stakeholders and it is important to continuously involve them as testing progresses as the criteria may need to be revised.

- **Plan and design tests**: Know the usage pattern of the application (if any), and come up with realistic usage scenarios including variability among the various scenarios. For example, if the application in question has a user registration module, how many users typically register for an account in a day? Do those registrations happen all at once, or are they spaced out? How many people frequent the landing page of the application within an hour? Questions such as these help to put things in perspective and design variations in the test plan. Having said that, there may be times where the application under test is new and so no usage pattern has been formed yet. At such times, stakeholders should be consulted to understand their business process and come up with as close to a realistic test plan as possible.

- **Prepare the test environment**: Configure the test environment, tools, and resources necessary to conduct the planned test scenarios. It is important to ensure that the test environment is instrumented for resource monitoring to help analyze results more efficiently. Depending on the company, a separate team might be responsible for setting up the test tools, while another may be responsible for configuring other aspects such as resource monitoring. In other organizations, a single team is responsible for setting up all aspects.

- **Record the test plan**: Using a testing tool, record the planned test scenarios. There are numerous testing tools available, both free and commercial that do the job quite well, each having their pros and cons.

  Such tools include HP Load Runner, NeoLoad, LoadUI, Gatling, WebLOAD, WAPT, Loadster, LoadImpact, Rational Performance Tester, Testing Anywhere, OpenSTA, Loadstorm, and so on. Some of these are commercial while others are not as mature or as portable or extendable as JMeter is. HP Load Runner, for example, is a bit pricey and limits the number of simulated threads to 250 without purchasing additional licenses. It does offer a much nicer graphical interface and monitoring capability though. Gatling is the new kid on the block, is free and looks rather promising. It is still in its infancy and aims to address some of the shortcomings of JMeter, including easier testing DSL (domain specific language) versus JMeter's verbose XML, nicer and more meaningful HTML reports, among others. Having said that, it still has only a tiny user base when compared with JMeter, and not everyone may be comfortable with building test plans in Scala, its language of choice. Programmers may find it more appealing.

  In this book, our tool of choice will be Apache JMeter to perform this step. That shouldn't be a surprise considering the title of the book.

- **Run the tests**: Once recorded, execute the test plans under light load and verify the correctness of the test scripts and output results. In cases where test or input data is fed into the scripts to simulate more realistic data (more on that in the later chapters), also validate the test data. Another aspect to pay careful attention to during test plan execution is the server logs. This can be achieved through the resource monitoring agents set up to monitor the servers. It is paramount to watch for warnings and errors. A high rate of errors, for example, could be indicative that something is wrong with the test scripts, application under test, system resource, or a combination of these.

- **Analyze results, report, and retest**: Examine the results of each successive run and identify areas of bottleneck that need addressing. These could be system, database, or application related. System-related bottlenecks may lead to infrastructure changes such as increasing the memory available to the application, reducing CPU consumption, increasing or decreasing thread pool sizes, revising database pool sizes, and reconfiguring network settings. Database-related bottlenecks may lead to analyzing database I/O operations, top queries from the application under test, profiling SQL queries, introducing additional indexes, running statistics gathering, changing table page sizes and locks, and a lot more. Finally, application-related changes might lead to activities such as refactoring application components, reducing application memory consumption and database round trips. Once the identified bottlenecks are addressed, the test(s) should then be rerun and compared with previous runs. To help better track what change or group of changes resolved a particular bottleneck, it is vital that changes are applied in an orderly fashion, preferably one at a time. In other words, once a change is applied, the same test plan is executed and the results compared with a previous run to see if the change made had any improved or worsened effect on results. This process repeats until the performance goals of the project have been met.

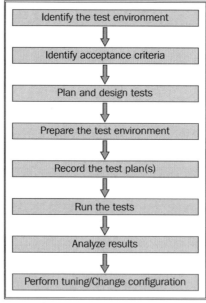

Performance testing core activities

Performance testing is usually a collaborative effort between all parties involved. Parties include business stakeholders, enterprise architects, developers, testers, DBAs, system admins, and network admins. Such collaboration is necessary to effectively gather accurate and valuable results when conducting testing. Monitoring network utilization, database I/O and waits, top queries, and invocation counts, for example, helps the team find bottlenecks and areas that need further attention in ongoing tuning efforts.

Performance testing and tuning

There is a strong relationship between performance testing and tuning, in the sense that one often leads to the other. Often, end-to-end testing unveils system or application bottlenecks that are regarded as incompatible with project target goals. Once those bottlenecks are discovered, the next step for most teams is a series of tuning efforts to make the application perform adequately.

Such efforts normally include but are not limited to:

- Configuring changes in system resources
- Optimizing database queries
- Reducing round trips in application calls; sometimes leading to re-designing and re-architecting problematic modules
- Scaling out application and database server capacity
- Reducing application resource footprint
- Optimizing and refactoring code; including eliminating redundancy, and reducing execution time

Tuning efforts may also commence if the application has reached acceptable performance but the team wants to reduce the amount of system resources being used, decrease volume of hardware needed, or further increase system performance.

After each change (or series of changes), the test is re-executed to see whether performance has increased or declined as a result of the changes. The process will be continued until the performance results reach acceptable goals. The outcome of these test-tuning circles normally produces a baseline.

Baselines

Baseline is a process of capturing performance metric data for the sole purpose of evaluating the efficacy of successive changes to the system or application. It is important that all characteristics and configurations except those specifically being varied for comparison remain the same, in order to make effective comparisons as to which change (or series of changes) is the driving result towards the targeted goal. Armed with such baseline results, subsequent changes can be made to system configuration or application and testing results compared to see whether such changes were relevant or not. Some considerations when generating baselines include:

- They are application specific
- They can be created for system, application, or modules
- They are metrics/results
- They should not be over generalized
- They evolve and may need to be redefined from time to time
- They act as a shared frame of reference
- They are reusable
- They help identify changes in performance

Load and stress testing

Load testing is the process of putting demand on a system and measuring its response; that is, determining how much volume the system can handle. **Stress testing** is the process of subjecting the system to unusually high loads far beyond its normal usage pattern to determine its responsiveness. These are different from performance testing whose sole purpose is to determine the response and effectiveness of a system; that is, how fast is the system. Since load ultimately affects how a system responds, performance testing is almost always done in conjunction with stress testing.

JMeter to the rescue

In the previous section, we covered the fundamentals of conducting a performance test. One of the areas performance testing covers is **testing tools**. Which testing tool do you use to put the system and application under load? There are numerous testing tools available to perform this operation, from free to commercial solutions. However, our focus in this book will be on Apache JMeter, a free open source, cross platform desktop application from The Apache Software Foundation. JMeter has been around since 1998 according to historic change logs on its official site, making it a mature, robust, and reliable testing tool. Cost may also have played a role in its wide adoption. Small companies usually may not want to foot the bill for commercial testing tools, which often still place restrictions on how many concurrent users one can spin off, for example. My first encounter with JMeter was exactly as a result of this. I worked in a small shop that had paid for a commercial testing tool, but during the course of testing, we had overrun the licensing limits of how many concurrent users we needed to simulate for realistic test plans. Since JMeter was free, we explored it and were quite delighted with the offerings and the sheer number of features we got for free.

Here are some of its features:

- Performance test of different server types including web (HTTP and HTTPS), SOAP, database, LDAP, JMS, mail, and native commands or shell scripts
- Complete portability across various operating systems
- Full multithreading framework allowing concurrent sampling by many threads and simultaneous sampling of different functions by separate thread groups
- GUI (Graphical User Interface)
- HTTP proxy recording server
- Caching and offline analysis/replaying of test results
- Highly extensible
- Live view of results as testing is being conducted

JMeter allows multiple concurrent users to be simulated on the application allowing you to work towards most of the target goals mentioned earlier in the chapter, such as attaining baseline, identifying bottlenecks, and so on.

It will help answer questions such as:

- Will the application still be responsive if 50 users are accessing it concurrently?

- How reliable will it be under a load of 200 users?

- How much system resources will be consumed under a load of 250 users?

- What is throughput going to look like when 1000 users are active in the system?

- What is the response time for the various components in the application under load?

JMeter, however, should not be confused with a browser (more on that in *Chapter 2, Recording Your First Test* and *Chapter 3, Submitting Forms*). It doesn't perform all the operations supported by browsers; in particular, JMeter does not execute JavaScript found in HTML pages, nor does it render HTML pages the way a browser does. It does give you the ability to view request responses as HTML through one of its many listeners, but the timings are not included in any samples. Furthermore, there are limitations as to how many users can be spun on a single machine. These vary depending on the machine specifications (for example, memory and processor speed) and the test scenarios being executed. In our experience, we have mostly been able to successfully spin off 250-450 users on a single machine with 2.2GHz processor and 8 GB of RAM.

Up and running with JMeter

Now let's get up and go running with JMeter, beginning with its installation.

Installation

JMeter comes as a bundled archive so it is super easy to get started with it. Those working in corporate environments behind a firewall or machines with non-admin privileges appreciate this more. To get started, grab the latest binary release by pointing your browser to `http://jmeter.apache.org/download_jmeter.cgi`. At the time of writing, the current release version is 2.9. The download site offers the bundle as both `zip` and `tar`. In this book, we will use the ZIP option, but feel free to download the TGZ if that's your preferred way of grabbing archives.

Once downloaded, extract the archive to a location of your choice. Throughout this book, the location you extracted the archive to will be referred to as JMETER_HOME.

Provided you have a JDK/JRE correctly installed and a JAVA_HOME environment variable set, you are all set and ready to run!

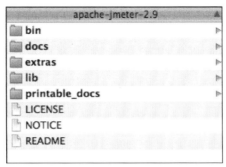

The JMETER_HOME folder structure

The following are some of the folders in the apache-jmeter-2.9 folder, as shown in the preceding screenshot:

- bin: This folder contains executable scripts to run and perform other operations in JMeter
- docs: This folder contains a comprehensive user guide
- extras: This folder contains miscellaneous items including samples illustrating using Apache Ant build tool (http://ant.apache.org/) with JMeter and bean shell scripting
- lib: This is the folder utility JAR files needed by JMeter (you may add additional JARs here to use from within JMeter — more on that later)
- printable_docs: This is the printable documentation

Installing Java JDK

Follow these steps to install Java JDK:

1. Go to http://www.oracle.com/technetwork/java/javase/downloads/index.html.

2. Download Java JDK (not JRE) compatible with the system you will be using to test.

3. Double-click on the executable and follow the on-screen instructions.

On Windows systems, the default location for the JDK is under `Program Files`. While there is nothing wrong with that, the issue is that the folder name contains a space, which can sometimes be problematic when attempting to set PATH and run programs such as JMeter from the command line. With that in mind, it is advisable to change the default location to something such as `C:\tools\jdk`.

Setting JAVA_HOME

The steps to set up the `JAVA_HOME` environment variable for Windows and Unix operating systems are explained next.

On Windows

For illustrative purposes, we assume you have installed Java JDK at `C:\tools\jdk`:

1. Go to **Control Panel**.
2. Click on **System**.
3. Click on **Advance System settings**.
4. Add the **Environment variable** as follows:
   - **Value**: `JAVA_HOME`
   - **Path**: `C:\tools\jdk`
5. Locate **Path** (under **System variables**; bottom half of the screen).
6. Click on **Edit**.
7. Append `%JAVA_HOME%/bin` to the end of the existing path value (if any).

On Unix

For illustrative purposes, we assume you have installed Java JDK at `/opt/tools/jdk`:

1. Open a terminal window.
2. Export `JAVA_HOME=/opt/tools/jdk`.
3. Export `PATH=$PATH:$JAVA_HOME`.

It is advisable to set this in your shell profile settings such as `.bash_profile` (for Bash users) or `.zshrc` (for zsh users) so you won't have to set it for each new terminal window you open.

Running JMeter

Once installed, the `bin` folder under JMETER_HOME folder contains all the executable scripts that can be run. Based on which operating system you installed JMeter on, you either execute the shell scripts (`.sh`) for Unix/Linux flavored operating systems or their batch (`.bat`) counterparts on Windows operating systems.

 JMeter files are saved as XML files with a `.jmx` extension. We refer to them as test scripts or JMX files in this book.

These scripts include:

- `jmeter.sh`: This script launches JMeter GUI (the default)

- `jmeter-n.sh`: This script launches JMeter in non-GUI mode (takes a JMX file as input)

- `jmeter-n-r.sh`: This script lauches JMeter in non-GUI mode, remotely

- `jmeter-t.sh`: This script opens a JMX file in the GUI

- `jmeter-server.sh`: This script starts JMeter in server mode (this will be started on the master node when testing with multiple machines remotely. More on that in *Chapter 6, Distributed Testing*).

- `mirror-server.sh`: This script runs the mirror server for JMeter

- `shutdown.sh`: This script gracefully shuts down a running non-GUI instance

- `stoptest.sh`: This script abruptly shuts down a running non-GUI instance

To start JMeter, open a terminal shell, change to the JMETER_HOME\bin folder and run the following:

- On Unix/Linux:

  ./jmeter.sh

- On Windows:

  jmeter.bat

After a short moment, you should see the JMeter GUI (as shown in the following screenshot). Take a moment to explore the GUI. Hover over each icon to see a short description of what it does. The Apache JMeter team has done an excellent job with the GUI. Most icons are very similar to what you are used to, which helps ease the learning curve for new adapters. Some of the icons, for example, stop, and shutdown, are disabled until a scenario/test is being conducted. In the next chapter, we will explore the GUI in more detail as we record our first test script.

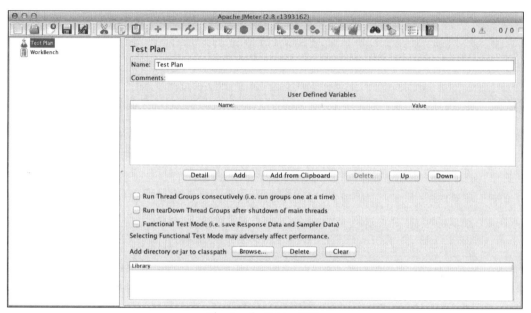

The Apache JMeter GUI

Command-line options

Running JMeter with incorrect option provides you with usage info. The options provided are as follows:

```
./jmeter.sh -

  -h, --help
    print usage information and exit
  -v, --version
    print the version information and exit
  -p, --propfile <argument>
    the jmeter property file to use
  -q, --addprop <argument>
```

```
   additional JMeter property file(s)
 -t, --testfile <argument>
   the jmeter test(.jmx) file to run
 -l, --logfile <argument>
   the file to log samples to
 -j, --jmeterlogfile <argument>
   jmeter run log file (jmeter.log)
 -n, --nongui
   run JMeter in nongui mode
```

The previous code snippet (non-exhaustive list) is what you might see if you did the same. We will explore some, but not all of these options as we go through the book.

JMeter's Classpath

Since JMeter is 100 percent pure Java, it comes packed with functionality to get most test cases scripted. However, there might come a time when you need to pull in a functionality provided by a third-party library or one developed by yourself, which is not present by default. As such, JMeter provides two directories where such third-party libraries can be placed to be autodiscovered in its classpath.

- JMETER_HOME\lib: This is used for utility JARs

- JMETER_HOME\lib\ext: This is used for JMeter components and add-ons. All custom developed JMeter components should be placed in the lib\ext folder, while third-party libraries (JAR files), should reside in the lib folder.

Configuring the proxy server

If you are working from behind a corporate firewall, you may need to configure JMeter to work with it by providing the proxy server host and port number. To do so, supply additional command-line parameters to JMeter when starting it up. Some of them are as follows:

- -H: Specifies the proxy server hostname or IP address

- -P: Specifies the proxy server port

- -u: Specifies the proxy server username if required

- -a: Specifies the proxy server password if required, for example:

  ```
  ./jmeter.sh -H proxy.server -P7567 -u username -a password
  ```

On Windows, run jmeter.bat instead.

Do not confuse the proxy server mentioned here with JMeter's built-in HTTP Proxy Server, which is used for recording HTTP or HTTPS browser sessions. We will be exploring that in the next chapter when we record our first test scenario.

Running in non-GUI mode

As described earlier, JMeter can run in non-GUI mode. This is needed for times when you are running remotely, or want to optimize your testing system by not taking the extra overhead cost of running the GUI. Normally, you will run the default (GUI), when recording your test scripts and running a light load but run in non-GUI mode for higher loads.

To do so, use the following command-line options:

- `-n`: This command-line option indicates to run in non-GUI mode
- `-t`: This command-line option specifies the name of the JMX test file
- `-l`: This command-line option specifies the name of the JTL file to log results to
- `-j`: This command-line option specifies the name of the JMeter run log file
- `-r`: This command-line option runs the test servers specified by the JMeter property `remote_hosts`
- `-R`: This command-line option runs the test on the specified remote servers (for example, `-Rserver1,server2`)

In addition, you can also use the `-H` and `-P` options to specify proxy server host and port, as we saw earlier:

```
./jmeter.sh -n -t test_plan_01.jmx -l log.jtl
```

Running in server mode

This is used when performing distributed testing; that is, using more testing servers to generate additional load on your system. JMeter will be kicked off in server mode on each remote server (slaves) and then a GUI on the master server is used to control the slave nodes. We will discuss this in detail when we dive into distributed testing in *Chapter 6, Distributed Testing*.

```
./jmeter-server.sh
```

Specify the `server.exitaftertest=true` JMeter property if you want the server to exit after a single test has been completed. It is set to false by default.

Overriding properties

JMeter provides two ways to override Java, JMeter, and logging properties. One way is to directly edit the `jmeter.properties`, which resides in the JMETER_HOME\ bin folder. We'll suggest you take a peek into this file and see the vast number of properties you can override. This is one of the things that make JMeter so powerful and flexible. On most occasions, you will not need to override the defaults, as they have sensible default values.

The other way to override these values is directly from the command line when starting JMeter.

The options available to you include:

- Define a Java system property value:

  ```
  -D<property name>=<value>
  ```

- Define a local JMeter property:

  ```
  -J<property name>=<value>
  ```

- Define a JMeter property to be sent to all remote servers:

  ```
  -G<property name>=<value>
  ```

- Define a file containing JMeter properties to be sent to all remote servers:

  ```
  -G<property file>
  ```

- Overriding a logging setting by setting a category to a given priority level:

  ```
  -L<category>=<priority>
  ./jmeter.sh -Duser.dir=/home/bobbyflare/jmeter_stuff \
      -Jremote_hosts=127.0.0.1 -Ljmeter.engine=DEBUG
  ```

 Since command-line options are processed after the logging system has been set up, any attempts to use the `-J` flag to update the `log_level` or `log_file` properties will have no effect.

Tracking errors during test execution

JMeter keeps track of all errors that occur during a test in a logfile named `jmeter.log` by default. The file resides in the folder from which JMeter was launched. The name of this log file, like most things, can be configured in `jmeter.properties` or via a command-line parameter (`-j <name_of_log_file>`). When running the GUI, the error count is indicated in the top-right corner, to the left of the number of threads running for the test. Clicking on it reveals the log file contents directly at the bottom of the GUI. The log file provides an insight into what exactly is going on in JMeter when your tests are being executed and helps determine the cause of error(s) when they occur.

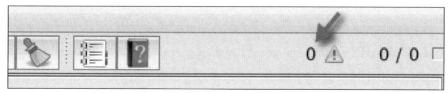

The JMeter GUI error count/indicator

Configuring JMeter

Should you need to customize the default values for JMeter, you can do so by editing the `jmeter.properties` file in the JMETER_HOME\bin folder, or making a copy of that file, renaming it to something different (for example, `my-jmeter.properties`), and specifying that as a command-line option when starting JMeter.

Some options you can configure include:

- `xml.parser`: It specifies a custom XML parser implementation. The default value is `org.apache.xerces.parsers.SAXParser`. It is not mandatory. If you find the provided SAX parser buggy for some of your use cases, this provides you the option to override it with another implementation. You could, for example, use `javax.xml.parsers.SAXParser` provided the right JARs exist on your instance of the JMeter classpath.

- `remote_hosts`: It is a comma-delimited list of remote JMeter hosts (or `host:port` if required). When running JMeter in a distributed environment, list the machines where you have JMeter remote servers running. This will allow you to control those servers from this machine's GUI. This applies only while doing distributed testing and is not mandatory. More on this in *Chapter 6, Distributed Testing*.

- `not_in_menu`: It is a list of components you do not want to see in JMeter's menus. Since JMeter has quite a number of components, you may wish to restrict it to show only components you are interested in or those you use regularly. You may list their classname or their class label (the string that appears in JMeter's UI) here, and they will no longer appear in the menus. The defaults are fine, and in our experience we have never had to customize this, but we list it here so that you are aware of its existence. It is not mandatory.

- `user.properties`: It specifies the name of the file containing additional JMeter properties. These are added after the initial property file, but before the `-q` and `-J` options are processed. It is not mandatory. User properties can be used to provide additional classpath configurations such as plugin paths, via the `search_paths` attribute, and utility JAR paths via the `user_classpath` attribute. In addition, these properties file can be used to fine-tune JMeter components' log verbosity.

    ○ `search_paths`: It specifies a list of paths (separated by `;`) that JMeter will search for JMeter add-on classes; for example, additional samplers. This is in addition to any JARs found in the `lib\ext` folder. It is not mandatory. This comes in handy, for example, when extending JMeter with additional plugins that you don't intend to install in the `JMETER_HOME\lib\ext` folder. You could use this to specify an alternate location on the machine to pick up the plugins. See *Chapter 5, Resource Monitoring*.

    ○ `user.classpath`: In addition to JARs in the `lib` folder, use this attribute to provide additional paths JMeter will search for utility classes. It is not mandatory.

- `system.properties`: It specifies the name of the file containing additional system properties for JMeter to use. These are added before the `-S` and `-D` options are processed. It is not mandatory. This typically provides you with the ability to fine-tune various SSL settings, key stores, and certificates.

    ○ `ssl.provider` : It specifies a custom SSL implementation, if ou don't want to use the built-in Java implementation. It is not mandatory. If for some reason, the default built-in Java implementation of SSL, which is quite robust, doesn't meet your particular usage scenario, this allows you to provide a custom one. In our experience, the default has always been sufficient.

The command-line options are processed in the following order of precedence:

- `-p profile` is optional. If present, it is loaded and processed.
- `jmeter.properties` is loaded and processed after any user provided custom properties file.
- `-j logfile` is optional. If present, it is loaded and processed after the `jmeter.properties` file.
- Logging is initialized.
- `user.properties` is loaded (if any).
- `system.properties` is loaded (if any).
- All other command-line options are processed.

Summary

In this chapter, we have covered the fundamentals of performance testing. We also learned key concepts and activities surrounding performance testing in general. In addition, we installed JMeter, learned how to get it fully running on a machine and explored some of the configurations available with it. We explored some of the options that make JMeter a great tool of choice for your next performance testing engagement. These include the fact that it is free and mature, open-sourced, easily extensible and customizable, completely portable across various operating systems, has a great-plugin ecosystem, large user community, built-in GUI, and recording and validating test scenarios among others. In comparison with the other tools for performance testing, JMeter holds its own. In the next chapter, we will record our first test scenario and dive deeper into JMeter.

2
Recording Your First Test

JMeter comes with a built-in proxy server (`http://en.wikipedia.org/wiki/Proxy_server`) to aid you record test plans. The proxy server, once configured, watches your actions as you perform operations on a website, creates test sample objects for them and eventually stores them in your test plan; that is, a JMX file. JMeter gives you the option of creating test plans manually, but this is mostly impractical for recording most testing scenarios. You will save a whole lot of time using the proxy recorder, as you will see in a bit.

So without further ado, let's record our first test! For this, we will record the browsing of JMeter's own official website as a user would normally do. For the proxy server to be able to watch your actions, it will need to be configured. This entails two steps:

1. Setting up the HTTP proxy server within JMeter.
2. Setting the proxy in the browser.

Configuring the JMeter HTTP proxy server

The first step is to configure the proxy server in JMeter. To do this, we follow the following steps:

1. Start JMeter.

2. Add a Thread Group by right-clicking on **Test Plan** and navigating to **Add | Threads (User) | Thread Group**.

3. Add the **HTTP Proxy Server** element by right-clicking on **WorkBench** and navigating to **Add | Non-Test Elements | HTTP Proxy Server**.

4. Change the port to 7000 (under **Global Settings**).You can use a different port if you want to. What is important is to choose a port that is not currently used by an existing process on the machine. The default is 8080.

5. Go to **Test Plan | Thread Group** under **HTTP Proxy Server** (under the **Test plan content | Target Controller** section). This allows the recorded actions to be targeted to the thread group we created in step 2.

6. Choose the option **Put each group in a new transaction controller** under **HTTP Proxy Server** (under **Test plan content | Grouping** section). This allows you to group a series of requests as constituting a page load. We will see more on this topic later.

7. Click on **Add Suggested Excludes** (under **URL Patterns to Exclude**). This instructs the proxy server to bypass recording requests of a series of elements which are not relevant to test execution. These include JavaScript files, stylesheets, and images. Thankfully, JMeter provides a handy button that excludes the often-excluded elements.

8. Click on the **Start** button at the bottom of the **HTTP Proxy Server** component.

With these settings, the proxy server will start on port 7000, monitor all requests going through that port, and record them to a test plan using the default recording controller. For details see the following screenshot:

Configuring the JMeter HTTP Proxy Server

Setting up your browser to use the proxy server

There are several ways to set up the browser of your choice to use the proxy server. We'll go over two of the most common ways, starting with our personal favorite, which is using a browser extension.

Using a browser extension

Google Chrome and Firefox have vibrant browser plugin ecosystems that allow you to extend the capabilities of your browser with each plugin you choose. For setting up a proxy, we really like **FoxyProxy** (`http://getfoxyproxy.org/`). It is a neat add-on to the browser that allows you to set up various proxy settings and toggle between them on the fly, without having to mess around with system settings on the machine. It really makes the work hassle free. Thankfully, FoxyProxy has a plugin for Internet Explorer, Chrome, and Firefox. If you are using any of those, you are in luck; go ahead and grab it!

Changing the system settings

For those who would rather configure the proxy natively on their operating system, we have provided the following steps for Windows and Mac OS.

On a Windows OS, perform the following steps to configure a proxy:

1. Click on **Start** and then on **Control Panel**.
2. Click on **Network and Internet**.
3. Click on **Internet Options**.
4. In the **Internet Options** dialog box, click on the **Connections** tab.
5. Click on the **LAN Settings** button.

6. To enable the use of a proxy server, check the box for **Use a proxy server for your LAN (These settings will not apply to dial-up or VPN connections)** as shown in the following screenshot:

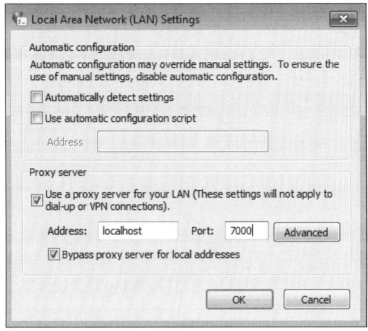

Manually setting up a proxy on Windows 7

1. In the proxy's **Address** box, enter `localhost` in the IP address.

2. In the **Port** textbox, enter `7000` (to match the port you set up for your JMeter proxy earlier).

3. If you want to bypass the proxy server for local IP addresses, select the **Bypass proxy server for local addresses** checkbox.

4. Click on **OK** to complete the proxy configuration process.

On a Mac OS, perform the following steps to configure a proxy:

1. Go to **System Preferences**.

2. Click on **Network**.

3. Click on the **Advanced...** button.

4. Go to the **Proxies** tab.

5. Check **Web Proxy (HTTP)**.

6. Under **Web Proxy Server**, enter `localhost`.

7. For port, enter `7000` (to match the port you set up for your JMeter proxy earlier).

8. Do the same for **Secure Web Proxy (HTTPS)**.

9. Click on **OK**.

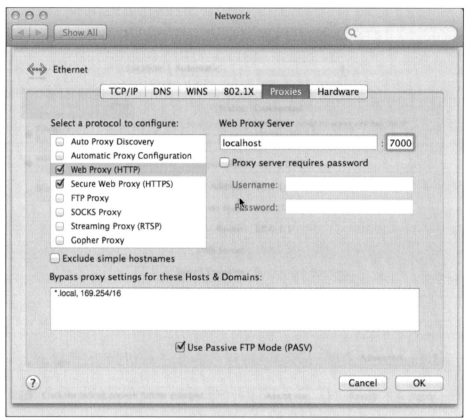

Manually setting up a proxy on Mac OS

For all other systems, please consult the related operating system's documentation.

Now that all of that is out of the way and the connections have been made, let's get to recording.

1. Point your browser to `http://jmeter.apache.org/`.

2. Click on the **Changes** link under **About**.

3. Click on the **User Manual** link under **User Manual**.

4. Stop the JMeter proxy server by clicking on the **Stop** button; it will not record any further activities.

5. If you have done everything correctly, your actions should have been recorded under the test plan.

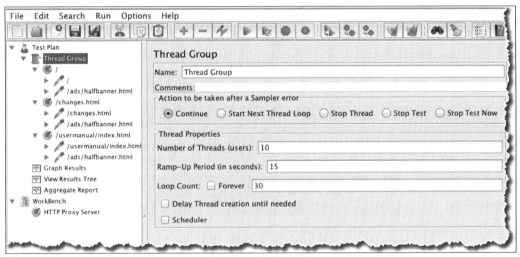

First recorded scenario

Congratulations! You have just recorded your first test plan. Admittedly, we have just scraped the surface of recording test plans, but we are off to a good start. We will record many more plans, even complex ones, as we proceed through the book.

Running your first recorded scenario

We can go right ahead and replay or run our recorded scenario now, but before that let's add a listener or two to give us feedback on the results of the execution. We will cover listeners in depth in *Chapter 5, Resource Monitoring*, when we discuss resource monitoring, but for now it is enough to know that they are components that show the results of the test run. There is no limit to the amount of listeners we can attach to a test plan, but we will often use only one or two.

For our test plan, let's add three listeners for illustrative purposes. Let's add the **Graph Results**, **View Results Tree**, and **Aggregate Report** listeners. Each gathers a different kind of metric that can help analyze performance test results.

1. Right-click on **Test Plan** and navigate to **Add | Listener | View Results Tree**.

2. Right-click on **Test Plan** and navigate to **Add | Listener | Aggregate Report**.

3. Right-click on **Test Plan** and navigate to **Add | Listener | Graph Results**.

Now that we can see more interesting data, let's change some settings at the thread group level.

1. Click on **Thread Group**.

2. Under **Thread Properties**, enter the following values:

   ○ **Number of Threads (users)**: 10

   ○ **Ramp-Up Period (in seconds)**: 15

   ○ **Loop Count**: 30

This will set up our test plan to run for 10 users, with all users starting their test within 15 seconds, and have each user perform the recorded scenario 30 times. Before we proceed with test execution, save the test plan by clicking on the Save icon.

Once saved, click on the Start icon (the green play icon on the menu) and watch the test run. As the test runs, you can click on **Graph Results** (or either of the other two) and watch the results gathering in real time. This is one of the many features of JMeter.

From the Aggregate Report listener, we can see that there were 600 requests made to both the **changes** and **usermanual** links. Also, we see that most users (**90% Line**) got very good responses - below 200 milliseconds for both. In addition, we see what the throughput is per second for the various links and that there was a 0.33 percent error rate on the **changes** link, meaning some requests to that link failed.

Label	# Samples	Average	Median	90% Line	Min	Max
/	600	134	125	159	107	360
/ads/halfbanne...	900	14	12	20	10	109
/changes.html	600	136	128	164	110	263
/usermanual/in...	600	133	126	160	108	348
TOTAL	2700	94	115	155	10	360

The Aggregate Report listener

Looking at the View Results Tree listener, we see exactly which **changes** link requests failed and the reasons for their failure. This can be valuable information to developers or system engineers in diagnosing the root cause of the errors.

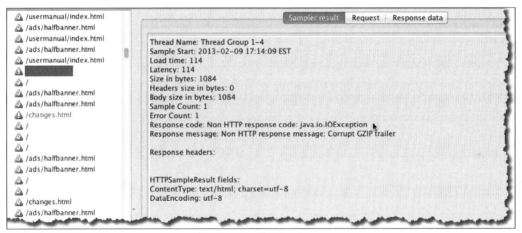

The View Results Tree listener

The Graph Results listener also gave a pictorial representation of what is seen in the View Results Tree listener in the preceding screenshot. If you clicked on it as the test was going on, you would have seen the graph get drawn in real time as the requests were coming in. The graph is self-explanatory, with lines representing the average, median, deviation, and throughput. **Average**, **Median**, and **Deviation** show average, median, and deviation of the number of samplers per minute respectively, while **Throughput** shows the average rate of network packets delivered over the network for our test run in bits per minute. Please consult the Web (for example, Wikipedia) for detailed explanation of these terms. The graph is also interactive and you can go ahead and uncheck/check any of the irrelevant/relevant data. For example, we mostly care about the average and throughput. Let's uncheck **Data**, **Median**, and **Deviation** and you will see that only the data plots for **Average** and **Throughput** remain. See the following screenshot for details:

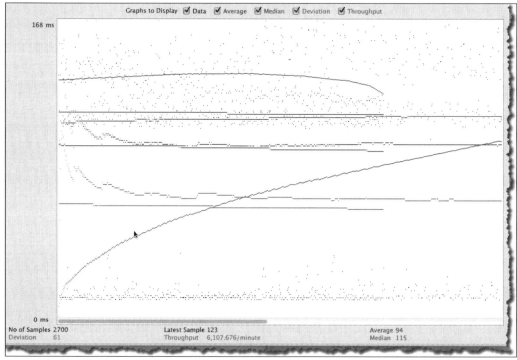

The Graph Results listener

With our little recorded scenario, you have seen some of the major components that constitute a JMeter test plan. Let's record another scenario, this time using another application that will allow us to enter form values. We will explore this in depth in the next chapter, but for now let's take a sneak peek.

We'll borrow a website created by the wonderful folks at Excilys, a company focused on delivering skills and services in IT (http://www.excilys.com/). It's a light banking web application created for illustrative purposes. Let's start a new test plan. Set up the proxy like we did previously, and start recording.

1. Point your browser to http://excilysbank.aws.af.cm/public/ login.html.

2. Enter the username and password into the login form as follows:
   - **Username**: user1
   - **Password**: password1

3. Click on the **Personal Checking** link.

4. Click on the **Transfers** tab.

5. Click on **My Accounts**.

6. Click on the **Joint Checking** link.

7. Click on the **Transfers** tab.

8. Click on the **Cards** tab.

9. Click on the **Operations** tab.

10. Click on the **Log out** button.

11. Stop the proxy server (click on the **Stop** button).

That concludes our recorded scenario. At this point, we could add listeners to gather results of our execution and then replay the recorded scenario as we did before. If we did, we would be in for a surprise. We would have several failed requests after login, since we did not include the component to manage sessions and cookies needed to successfully replay this scenario. Thankfully, JMeter has such a component and it is called **HTTP Cookie Manager**. This seemingly simple, yet powerful, component helps maintain an active session via HTTP cookies, once our client has established a connection with the server, after login. It ensures that a cookie is stored upon successful authentication and passed around for subsequent requests, hence allowing those to go through. Each JMeter thread (that is, user) has its own cookie storage area. This is vital since you wouldn't want a user gaining access to the site under another user's identity. This becomes more apparent when we test for websites requiring authentication and authorization (like the one we just recorded) for multiple users. So, let's add this to our test plan by right-clicking on **Test Plan** and navigating to **Add | Config Element | HTTP Cookie Manager**.

Once added, we can successfully run our test plan. At this point, we can simulate more load by increasing the number of threads at the Thread Group level. Let's go ahead and do that. If executed, the test plan will pass, but this is not realistic. We have just emulated one user and essentially repeated the process five times. All threads will use the credentials of user1, meaning that all threads log into the system as user1. That is not what we want. To make the test realistic, what we want is each thread authenticating as a different user of the application. In reality, your bank creates a unique user for you, and only you and your spouse will be privileged to see your account details. Your neighbor down the street, if he uses the same bank, can't get access to your account (at least we hope not!). So with that in mind, let's tweak the test to accommodate such a scenario.

We begin by adding a CSV Data Set Config component (go to **Test Plan | Add | Config Element | CSV Data Set Config**) to our test plan. Since it is expensive to generate unique random values at runtime due to high CPU and memory consumption, it is advisable to define those values upfront. The CSV Data Set Config component is used to read lines from a file and split them into variables that can then be used to feed input into the test plan. JMeter gives you a choice for the placement of this component within the test plan. You would normally add the component at the HTTP request level of the request that needs values fed from it. In our case, this will be the login HTTP request, where the username and password are entered. Another is to add it at the Thread Group level; that is, as a direct child of the Thread Group. If a particular data set is applied to only a Thread Group, it makes sense to add it at that level. The third place where this component can be placed is at the Test Plan root level. If a data set applies to all running threads, it makes sense to add it at the root level. In our opinion, this also makes your test plans more readable and maintainable as it is easier to see what is going on when inspecting or troubleshooting a test plan, since this component can easily be seen at the root level rather than being deeply nested at other levels. So for our scenario, let's add this at the Test Plan root level.

[You can always move the components around using drag-and-drop, even after adding them to the Test Plan.]

CSV Data Set Config

Name:	CSV Data Set Config
Comments:	

Configure the CSV Data Source

Filename:	users.txt
File encoding:	
Variable Names (comma-delimited):	
Delimiter (use '\t' for tab):	,
Allow quoted data?:	False
Recycle on EOF ?:	True
Stop thread on EOF ?:	False
Sharing mode:	All threads

CSV Data Set Config

Once added, the **Filename** entry is all that is needed if you have included headers in the input file. For example, if the input file is defined as such:

```
user, password, account_id
user1, password1, 1
```

If the **Variable Names** field is left blank, JMeter will use the first line of the input file as the variable names for the parameters. In cases where headers are not included, the variable names can be entered here. The other interesting setting here is **Sharing mode**. This defaults to **All threads**, meaning that all running threads will use the same set of data. So in cases where you have two threads running, Thread1 will use the first line as input data while Thread2 will use the second line. If the number of running threads exceeds the input data, entries will be reused from the top of the file, provided that **Recycle on EOF** is set to true (the default). The other options for sharing modes include **Current thread group** and **Current thread**. Use the former for cases where the data set is specific for a certain Thread Group and the latter for cases where the data set is specific to each thread. The other properties of the component are self-explanatory, and additional information about them can be found in JMeter's online user guide.

Now that the component is added, we need to parameterize the login HTTP request with the variable names defined in our file (or the csvconfig component), so that the values can be dynamically bound during test execution. We do that by changing the value of the username to ${user} and password to ${password} on the HTTP login request.

The values between the braces, ${ }, match the headers defined in the input file or the values specified in the Variable Names entry of the CSV Data Set Config component.

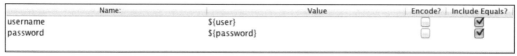

Name:	Value	Encode?	Include Equals?
username	${user}	☐	✔
password	${password}	☐	✔

Binding parameter values for the HTTP Requests

We can now run our test plan and it should work as before, only this time the values are dynamically bound through the configuration we have set up. So far, we have run it only for a single user. Let's change the thread group properties and run it for 10 users, with a ramp up of 30 seconds for 1 iteration. Now let's re-run our test. Examining the test results, we notice that some requests failed with a status code of 403 (http://en.wikipedia.org/wiki/HTTP_403), which is an access denied error. This is because we are trying to access an account that does not belong to the user that is logged in. In our sample, all users made a request for account number 1, which only one user (user1) is allowed to see. You can trace this by adding a View Results Tree listener to the test plan and returning the test.

If you closely examine some of the HTTP requests in the **Request** tab of the View Results Tree listener, you'll notice requests such as the following:

```
/private/bank/account/ACC1/operations.html
```

```
/private/bank/account/ACC1/year/2013/month/1/page/0/operations.json
```

. . .

Observant readers would have noticed that our input datafile also contains an account_id column. We can leverage this column to parameterize all requests containing account numbers to pick the right accounts for each user that is logged in.

To do that, we change the following line of code:

```
/private/bank/account/ACC1/operations.html
```

To this line of code:

```
/private/bank/account/ACC${account_id}/operations.html
```

And the following line of code:

```
/private/bank/account/ACC1/year/2013/month/1/page/0/operations.json
```

To this line of code:

```
/private/bank/account/ACC${account_id}/year/2013/month/1/page/0/
operations.json
```

And so on. Go ahead and do that for all such requests. Once completed, we can re-run our test plan, and this time things are logically correct and will work fine. You can also verify all work as expected after test execution, by examining the View Results Tree listener, clicking on some account requests URL, changing the response display from text to HTML, and you should see an account other than ACCT1.

This brings us to one more scenario to explore. Sometimes, it is useful to parse the response to get the required information, rather than have it sent as a column of the input data. The parsed response can be any textual format. These include JSON, HTML, TXT, XML, CSS, and so on. This could further help make your test plans more robust. In our preceding test plan, we could have leveraged this feature and parsed the response to get the required account number for users rather than sending it along as an input parameter. Once parsed and obtained, we can save and use the account number for other requests down the chain. Let's go ahead and record a new test plan as we did before. Save it under a new name. To aid us extract a variable from the response data, we will use one of JMeter's post processor components, **Regular Expression Extractor**. This component runs after each sample request in its scope, applying the regular expression and extracting the requested values. A template string is then generated and the result of this is stored into a variable name. This variable name is then used to parameterize, as in the case of the CSV Data Set Config component we saw earlier.

We'll add a Regular Expression Extractor component as a child element of the HTTP request to `/private/bank/accounts.html` just below the `/login` request. Unlike the CSV Data Set Config component we saw earlier, this component has to be placed directly as a child element of the request it will be acting on, since it's a post processor component. Its configuration should be as shown in the following screenshot:

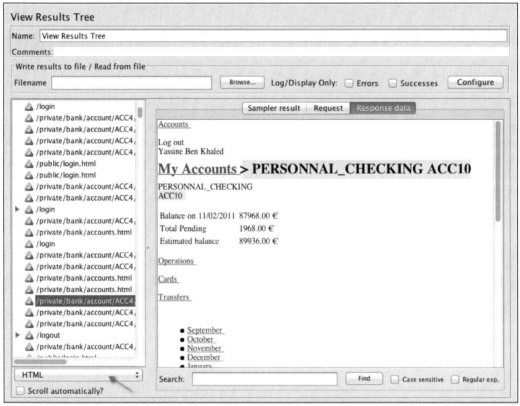

Using the View Results Tree to verify the response data

When configuring the Regular Expression Extractor component, use the following values for each of the indicated fields:

- **Apply to**: Main sample only
- **Response Field to check**: Body
- **Reference Name**: account_id
- **Regular Expression**: <td class="number">ACC(\d+)</td>
- **Template**: 1

- **Match No.**: 1
- **Default Value**: NOT_FOUND

The following screenshot shows what the component will look like with all of the entries filled out:

The Regular Expression Extractor configuration

Once configured, proceed to parameterize the other requests for accounts with the `${account_id}` variable just like we did earlier. At this point, we are able to re-run our test plan and get the exact same behavior and output as we did before when we were feeding in a data set, which also had `account_id` as a column. You have now seen two ways to get at the same information when building your own test plans. Though your use case will mostly vary from those we have examined here, the same principles will apply.

Here is a brief summary of the various configuration variables for the **Regular Expression Extractor** component:

Apply to: The default, **Main sample only**, is almost always okay, but there are times when the sample contains child samples that request embedded resources. The options allow you to target the main sample, subsamples, or both. The last option, **JMeter Variable**, allows assertions to be applied to the contents of the named variable.

Response field to check: This parameter specifies which field the regular expression should apply to. The options include:

- **Body** – The body of the response, excluding headers.
- **Body (unescaped)** – The body of the response with all HTML escape codes replaced.
- **Headers** – These may not be present for non-HTTP samples.
- **URL** – The URL of the request will be parsed with the regular expression.
- **Response code** – This can be 200, 403, or 500, meaning success, access denied, or internal server error, respectively. Check `http://en.wikipedia.org/wiki/HTTP_200#2xx_Success` for a complete list of various HTTP status codes.
- **Response Message** – This can be OK, Access Denied, or Internal server error.

Reference name: The variable name under which the parsed results will be saved. This is what will be used for parameterization.

Regular expression: Enter any valid regular expression. As a side note, JMeter regular expressions differ from their Perl counterparts. While all regular expressions in Perl must be enclosed within `//`, the same is invalid in JMeter. Regular expressions are a broad topic and you will see more of them throughout the course of the book, but we encourage you to read more at `http://en.wikipedia.org/wiki/Regular_expression`.

Template: The template used to create a string from the matches found. This is an arbitrary string with special elements to refer to a group; `$1$` refers to group 1, `$2$` to refers to `group 2`, and so on. `$0$` refers to whatever the expression matches. In our example, `$0$` would refer to `ACC<td class="number">ACC4</td>`, for example, and `$1$` refers to `ACC4`.

Match No.: This parameter indicates which match to use since the regular expression may match multiple times.

- `0` – This indicates that JMeter should use a match at random
- `n` – A positive number n means to select the *n*th match. The variables are set as follows:
    - `refName` – The value of the template

- ○ refName_gn – Where n is the groups for the match, for example, 1, 2, 3, and so on

- ○ refName_g – The number of groups in the regular expression (excluding 0)

 Note that when no matches occur, the refName_g0, refName_g1, and refName_g variables are all removed and the refName value is set to the default value, if present.

- Negative numbers can be used in conjunction with a ForEach controller. The variables are set as follows::

  - ○ refName_matchNr – This is the number of matches found. It could be 0.

  - ○ refName_n – Where n is the number of strings generated by the template, for example, 1, 2, 3, and so on.

  - ○ refName_n_gm – Where m is the number of groups for the match; for example, 0, 1, 2, and so on.

  - ○ refName – This is set to the default value (if present).

  - ○ refName_gn – This is not set.

Default value: If the regular expression doesn't match, the variable will be set to the default value set. This is an optional parameter, but we recommend you always set it as it helps debug and diagnose issues while creating your test plans.

Anatomy of a JMeter test

With the samples we have explored so far, we have seen a similar pattern emerging. We have seen what mostly constitutes a JMeter test plan. We'll use the remainder of this chapter to explore the anatomy and composition of JMeter tests.

Test Plan

Test Plan is the root element of the JMeter scripts and houses the other components, such as Threads, Config Elements, Timers, Pre-Processors, Post-Processors, Assertions, and Listeners. It also offers a few configurations of its own.

Firstly, it allows you to define user variables (name-value pairs) that can be used later in your scripts. It also allows us to configure how the Thread Groups it contains should run; that is, should Thread Groups run one at a time? As test plans evolve over time, you'll often have several Thread Groups contained within a test plan. This option allows you to determine how they run. By default, all Thread Groups are set to run concurrently. A useful option when getting started is **Functional Test Mode**. When checked, all server responses returned from each sample are captured. This can prove useful for small simulation runs, ensuring JMeter is configured correctly and the server is returning the expected results, but the downside is that JMeter will see performance degradation and file sizes could be huge. It is set to off by default and shouldn't be checked when conducting real test simulations. One more useful configuration is the ability to add third-party libraries that can be used to provide additional functionality for test cases. A time may come when your simulation needs additional libraries, those that are not bundled with JMeter by default. At such times, you can add those JARs via this configuration.

Thread Groups

Thread Groups, as we have seen, are the entry points for any test plan. They represent the number of threads/users JMeter will use to execute the test plan. All controllers and samplers for a test must reside under a Thread Group. Other elements, such as listeners, may be placed directly under a test plan in cases where you want them to apply to all Thread Groups or under a single Thread Group if they only pertain to that group. Thread Group configurations provide options to specify the number of threads that will be used for the test plan, how long it will take for all threads to become active (ramp up), and the number of times to execute the test. Each thread will execute the test plan completely independently of other threads. JMeter spins off multiple threads to simulate concurrent connections to the server. It is important that the ramp up be long enough to avoid too large a workload at the start of a test, as this can often lead to network saturation and invalidate test results. If the intention is to have x number of users active in the system, it is better to ramp up slowly and increase the number of iterations. A final option the configuration provides is the scheduler. This allows setting the start and end time of a test execution. For example, you can kick off a test to run during off-peak hours for exactly 1 hour.

Controllers

Controllers drive the processing of a test and come in two flavors: **sampler controllers** and **logical controllers**.

Sampler controllers send requests to a server. These include HTTP, FTP, JDBC, LDAP, and so on. JMeter has a comprehensive list of samplers, but we will mostly focus on HTTP request samplers in this book since we are focusing on testing web applications.

Logical controllers, on the other hand, allow the customization of the logic used to send the requests. For example, a `loop` controller can be used to repeat an operation a certain number of times, the `if` controller is for selectively executing a request, and the `while` controller for continuing to execute a request until some condition becomes false. As of the time of this writing, JMeter 2.9 came bundled with sixteen different controllers, each serving a different purpose.

Samplers

Samplers are components that help send requests to the server and wait for a response. Requests are processed in the order they appear in the tree. JMeter comes bundled with the following samplers:

- HTTP Request
- JDBC Request
- LDAP Request
- Soap/XML-RPC request
- Web service (SOAP) request
- FTP Request

Each of these has properties that can be tweaked further to suit your needs. In most cases, the default configurations are fine and can be used as is. You should consider adding assertions to samplers to perform basic validation on server responses. Often, during testing, the server may return a status code of 200, indicative of a successful request, but fail to display the page correctly. At such times, assertions can help to make sure that the request was indeed successful.

Logic controllers

Logic controllers help customize the logic used to decide how requests are sent to a server. They can modify requests, repeat requests, interleave requests, control the duration of requests' execution, switch requests, measure the overall time taken to perform requests, and so on. At the time of writing, JMeter comes bundled with a total of fifteen logic controllers. Please visit the online user guide (`http://jmeter.apache.org/usermanual/component_reference.html#logic_controllers`) to see a comprehensive list and details on each.

Test fragments

Test fragments are a special type of controller purely for code re-use within a test plan. They exist on the test plan tree at the same level as the Thread Group element and are not executed unless referenced either by an Include or Module Controller.

Listeners

Listeners are components that gather the results of a test run, allowing it to be further analyzed. In addition, listeners provide the ability to direct the data to a file for later use. Furthermore, they allow allows us to choose which fields to save and whether to use the CSV or XML format. All listeners save the same data, with the only difference being the way the data is presented on the screen. Listeners can be added anywhere in the test, including directly under the test plan. They will collect data only from the elements at or below their level.

JMeter comes bundled with about eighteen different listeners, all serving different purposes. Though you will often use only a handful of them, it is advisable to become familiar with what each offers to know when to use them.

Some listeners, such as `Assert Results`, `Comparison Assertion Visualizer`, `Distribution Graph`, `Graph Results`, `Spline Visualizer`, and `View Results`, in the tree are memory- and CPU-intensive and should not be used during actual test runs. They are okay to use for debugging and functional testing.

Timers

By default, JMeter threads send requests without pausing between each request. It is recommended that you specify a delay by adding one of the available timers to the Thread Group(s). This also helps make your test plans more realistic as real users couldn't possibly send requests at that speed. The timer causes JMeter to pause a certain amount of time before each sampler in its scope.

Assertions

Assertions are components that allow you to verify responses received from the server. In essence, they allow you to verify that the application is functioning correctly and that the server is returning the expected results. Assertions can be run on XML, JSON, HTTP, and other forms of responses returned from the server. Assertions can also be resource-intensive, so make sure you don't have them on for actual test runs.

Configuration elements

Configuration elements work closely with a sampler, enabling requests to be modified or added to. They are only accessible from inside the tree branch where you place the element. These elements include the HTTP Cookie Manager, HTTP Header Manager, and so on.

Pre-processor and post-processor elements

A pre-processor element, as the name implies, executes some actions prior to a request being made. Pre-processor elements are often used to modify the settings of a request just before it runs or to update variables that aren't extracted from the response text.

Post-processor elements execute some actions after a request has been made. They are often used to process response data and extract values from it.

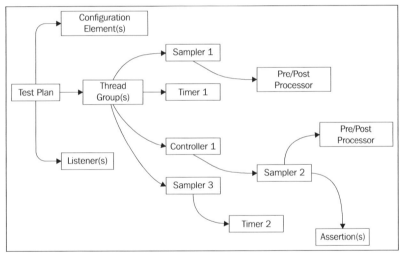

Anatomy of a JMeter test

Summary

We have covered quite a lot in this chapter. We have learned how to configure JMeter and our browsers to help record test plans. In addition, we have learned about some built-in components that can help us feed data into our test plan and/or extract data from server responses. In addition, we have learned what composes a JMeter test plan and got a good grasp on those components. In the next chapter, we will dive deeper into form submission and explore more JMeter components.

3
Submitting Forms

In this chapter, we'll expand on the foundations we started building in *Chapter 2, Recording Your First Test*, and dive deeper into submitting forms in greater detail. While most of the forms you encounter while recording test plans might be simple in nature, some are a whole different beast and require you to pay them more careful attention. For example, more and more websites are embracing **RESTful** web services, and as such, you would mainly interact with JSON objects when recording or executing test plans for such applications. Another area of interest will be recording applications that make use of AJAX heavily to accomplish business functionality. Google, for one, is known to be a mastermind at this. Most of their products, including Search, Gmail, Maps, YouTube, and so on, use AJAX extensively. Occasionally, you might have to deal with XML response data; for example, extracting parts of it to use for samples further down the chain in your test plan. You might also come across cases when you need to upload a file to the server or download one from it.

For all these and more, we will explore some practical examples in this chapter and gain some helpful insights as to how to deal with these scenarios when you come across them as you prepare your test plans.

Capturing simple forms

We have already encountered a variation of form submission in *Chapter 2, Recording Your First Test*, when we submitted a login form to authenticate with the server. The form had two text fields for username and password respectively. That's a good start. Most websites requiring authentication will have a similar feel to them. HTML forms, however, span a whole range of other input types. These include checkboxes, radio buttons, select and multiselect drop-down lists, text areas, file uploads, and so on. In this section, we take a look at handling other HTML input types.

We have created a sample application we will be using throughout most of this chapter to illustrate some of the concepts we will be discussing. The application can be reached at `http://jmeterbook.aws.af.cm`. Take a minute to browse around and take it for a manual spin so as to have an idea what the test scripts we record will be doing.

Handling checkboxes

Capturing checkbox submission is similar to that of capturing textbox submissions, which we encountered earlier in *Chapter 2, Recording Your First Test*. Depending on the use case, there might be one or more related/unrelated checkboxes on a form. Let's run through a scenario for illustrative purposes. With your JMeter proxy server running and capturing your actions, perform the following steps:

1. Go to `http://jmeterbook.aws.af.cm/form1/create`.
2. Enter a name in the textbox.
3. Check off a hobby or two.
4. Click on **Submit**.

At this point, if you examine the recorded test plan, the `/form1/submit` post request has parameters for the following:

- `name`: This represents the value entered in the textbox
- `hobbies`: You can have one or more depending on the number of hobbies you checked on
- `submit`: This is the value of the **Submit** button

We can then build upon the test plan by adding a CSV Data Set Config to the mix to allow us to feed different values for the names and hobbies (see `handling-checkboxes.jmx`). Finally, we can expand the test plan further by parsing the response from the `/form1/create` sample to determine what hobbies are available on the form using a post processor element (for example, the regular expression extractor) and then randomly choosing one or more of them to submit. I'll leave that as an exercise for the reader. Handling the multiselect option is no different from this.

Handling radio buttons

Radio buttons are normally used as option fields on a web page; that is, they are normally grouped together to present a series of choices to the user, allowing them to select one per group. Things such as marital status, favorite food, and polls are practical uses of them. Capturing their submission is quite similar to dealing with checkboxes, except that we will have just one entry per submission for each radio group. Our sample at `http://jmeterbook.aws.af.cm/radioForm/index` has only one radio group, allowing users to identify their marital status. Hence, after recording this, we will only have one entry submission for a user.

1. Go to `http://jmeterbook.aws.af.cm/radioForm/index`.
2. Enter a name in the textbox.
3. Pick a marital status.
4. Click on **Submit**.

Viewing the HTML source of the page (right-click anywhere on the page and select **View Source**) will normally get you the "IDs" the server is expecting back for each option presented on the page. Armed with that information, we can expand our input test data, allowing us to run this same scenario for more users with varying data. As always, you can use a post-processor component to further eliminate the need to send the radio button IDs in your input feed. Handling a drop-down list is no different to this scenario. Handling all other forms of HTML input types; for example, text and text area fall under the categories we have explored thus far.

Handling file uploads

You may encounter situations where uploading a file to the server is part of the functionality of the system under testing. JMeter can also help in this regard. It comes with a built-in multipart/form-data option on post requests, which is needed by HTML to correctly process file uploads. In addition to checking the option to make a post request multipart, you will need to specify the absolute path of the file, in cases where the file you are uploading is not within JMeter's `bin` directory, or the relative path in cases where the file resides within JMeter's `bin` directory. Let's record a scenario illustrating this:

1. Go to `http://jmeterbook.aws.af.cm/uploadForm`.
2. Enter a name in the textbox.

3. Choose a file to upload by clicking on the **Choose File** button.

4. Click on **Submit**.

 Note that files to be uploaded can't be larger than 1 MB.

Depending on the location of the file you choose, you might encounter an error similar to the following:

```
java.io.FileNotFoundException: Argentina.png (No such file or directory)
  at java.io.FileInputStream.open(Native Method)
  at java.io.FileInputStream.<init>(FileInputStream.java:120)
  at org.apache.http.entity.mime.content.FileBody.writeTo(FileBody.java:92)
  at org.apache.jmeter.protocol.http.sampler.HTTPHC4Impl$ViewableFileBody.writeTo(HTTPHC4Impl.java:773)
```

Do not be alarmed! This is because JMeter is expecting to find the file in its `bin` directory. You will have to either tweak the file location in the recorded script to point to the absolute path of the file or place it in the `bin` directory or a subdirectory. For the sample packaged with the book, we have opted to place the files in a subdirectory of the `bin` directory (`$JMETER_HOME/bin/samples/images`). Examine the file `handling-file-uploads.jmx`.

Handling file downloads

Another common situation you may encounter will be testing a system that has file download capabilities exposed as a function to its users. Users, for example, might download reports, user manuals, and documentation from a website. Knowing how much strain this can put on the server could be an area of interest to stakeholders. JMeter provides the ability to record and test such scenarios. As an example, let's record a user retrieving a PDF tutorial from JMeter's website.

1. Go to `http://jmeterbook.aws.af.cm/`.

2. Click on the **Handling File Downloads** link.

3. Click on the **Access Log Tutorial** link.

This should stream a PDF file to your browser. You could add a View Results Tree listener and examine the response output after playing back the recording. You could also add a Save Responses to file listener and have JMeter save the contents of the response to a file you can later inspect. This is the route we have opted for in the sample recorded with the book. Files will be created in the `bin` directory of JMeter's installation directory. See `handling-file-downloads-1.jmx`. Also, using a Save Responses to file listener is useful for cases when you would like to capture the response, in this case a file, and feed it to other actions further on in the test scenario. For example, we could have saved the response and used it to upload the file to another section of the same server or a different server entirely.

Posting JSON data

REST (REpresentational State Transfer) is a simple stateless architecture that generally runs over HTTP/HTTPS. Requests and responses are built around the transfer of representations of resources. It emphasizes interactions between clients and services by providing a limited number of operations (GET, POST, PUT, and DELETE). GET fetches the current state of a resource, POST creates a new resource, PUT updates an existing resource, and DELETE destroys the resource. Flexibility is provided by assigning resources their own unique universal resource indicators (URIs). Since each operation has a specific meaning, REST avoids ambiguity. In modern times, the typical object structure passed between client and server is JSON. More information about REST can be found at `http://en.wikipedia.org/wiki/REST`.

When dealing with websites that expose RESTful services in one form or another, you will most likely have to interact with JSON data in some way. Such websites may provide means to create, update, and delete data on the server via posting JSON data. URLs could also be designed to return existing data in JSON format. This happens even more in most modern websites, which use AJAX to an extent, as we use JSON mostly when interacting with AJAX. In all such scenarios, you will need to be able to capture and post data to the server using JMeter. JSON, also known as **JavaScript Object Notation**, is a text-based open standard designed for human readable data interchange. You can find out more information about it at `http://en.wikipedia.org/wiki/JSON` and `http://www.json.org/`. For this book, it will suffice to know what the structure of a JSON object looks like. Here are some examples:

```
{"empNo": 109987, "name": "John Marko", "salary": 65000}
```

And:

```
[{"id":1,"dob":"09-01-1965","firstName":"Barry", "lastName":"White",
"jobs":[{"id":1,"description":"Doctor"}, {"id":2,"description":"Firem
an"}]}]
```

Some basic rules of thumb when dealing with JSON are as follows:

- `[]` – indicates a list of objects
- `{}` – indicates an object definition
- `"key": "value"` – define string values of an object, under a desired key
- `"key": value` – define integer values of an object, under a desired key

So the first example we saw shows an employee object, with employee number `109987`, whose name is `John Marko`, and who earns `$65,000`. The second sample shows a person named `Barry White`, born on 9/1/1965, who is both a doctor and fireman.

Now that we have covered a sample JSON structure, let's examine how JMeter can help with posting JSON data. The example website provides a URL to save the `Person` object. A person has a first name, last name, and date of birth attributes. In addition, a person can hold multiple jobs. So a valid JSON structure to store a person might look like the following code:

```
{"firstName":"Malcom", "lastName":"Middle", "dob": "2/2/1965",
"jobs":[{"id": 1, "id": 2}]}
{"firstName":"Sarah", "lastName":"Martz", "dob": "3/7/1971"}
```

Instead of recording, we will manually construct the test scenario for this case; we have intentionally not provided a form to save a person's entry so as to give you hands-on practice in writing test plans for such scenarios.

1. Launch JMeter.
2. Add a Thread Group to the **Test Plan** by right-clicking on **Test Plan** and navigate to **Add | Threads (Users) | Thread Group**.
3. Add a HTTP Request Sampler to the **Thread Group** by right-clicking on **Thread Group** and navigate to **Add | Sampler | HTTP Request**.
4. Under **HTTP Request**, change **Implementation** to **HttpClient4**.
5. Fill in the properties of the **HTTP Request** Sampler as:
    ◦ **Server Name or IP**: `jmeterbook.aws.af.cm`
    ◦ **Method**: `POST`
    ◦ **Path**: `/person/save`

6. Under **Send Parameters with Request**, click on **Add** and fill in the attributes as follows:

    ○ **Name**: (leave blank)

    ○ **Value**: `{"firstName":"Bob", "lastName":"Jones", "jobs":[{"id":"3"}]}`

7. Add an HTTP Header Manager to the **HTTP Request Sampler** (right-click on **HTTP Request Sampler** | **Add** | **Config Element** | **HTTP Header Manager**).

    1. Add an attribute to **HTTP Header Manager** by clicking on it, and clicking on the **Add** button

    ○ **Name**: `Content-Type`

    ○ **Value**: `application/json`

8. Add a View Results Tree listener to the **Thread Group** by right-clicking on **Thread Group** and navigate to **Add** | **Listener** | **View Results Tree**.

9. Save the **Test Plan**.

If you have done everything correctly, your **HTTP Request** Sampler should look like the following screenshot:

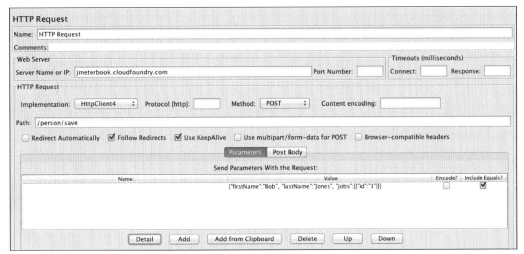

Configuring the HTTP Request Sampler to post JSON

Now you should be able to run the test, and if all was correctly set, Bob Jones should now be saved on the server. You can verify that by examining the View Results Tree listener. The request should be green and in the **Response data** tab, you should see Bob Jones listed as one of the entries returned. Even better yet, you could view the last ten stored entries in the browser directly at `http://jmeterbook.aws.af.cm/person/list`.

Of course all other tricks we have learned thus far apply here as well. We can use a CSV Data Config element to parameterize the test and have variation in our data input. See *posting-json.jmx* for that. Regarding input data variation, since jobs are optional for this input set, it might make sense to parameterize the whole JSON string read from input feed to give you more variation.

For example, you could replace the value with `${json}`, and have the input CSV Data have entries such as:

```
json
{"firstName":"Malcom", "lastName":"Middle", "dob": "1/2/1971",
"jobs":[{"id": 1, "id": 2}]}
{"firstName":"Sarah", "lastName":"Martz", "dob": "6/9/1982"}
```

We'll leave that as an exercise for you. Although simplistic in nature, what we have covered here should give you all of the information you need to post JSON data when recording your test plans.

When dealing with RESTful requests in general, it helps to have some tools handy to examine requests, inspect responses, and view network latency, among many others. The following is a list of handy tools that could help:

- **Firebug** (an add-on that is available with Firefox, Chrome, and IE): `http://getfirebug.com/`

- **Chrome developer tools**: `https://developers.google.com/chrome-developer-tools/`

- **Advance REST Client** (the Chrome browser extension): `http://bit.ly/15BEKlV`

- **REST Client** (the Firefox browser add-on): `http://mzl.la/h8YMlz`

Reading JSON data

Now that we know how to post JSON data, let's take a brief look at how to consume it in JMeter. Depending on the use case, you might find yourself dealing more with reading JSON than posting it. JMeter provides a number of ways to digest this information, store it if needed, and use it further down the chain in your test plans. Let's start with a simple use case. The example website has a link that provides details of the last ten person entries stored on the server. It is available at `http://jmeterbook.aws.af.cm/person/list`.

If we were to process the JSON response and use the first and last name further down the chain, we could use a Regular Expression Extractor post processor to extract those. Let's create a test plan to do just that.

1. Launch JMeter.

2. Add a Thread Group to the **Test Plan** (right-click on **Test Plan** and navigate to **Add | Threads (Users) | Thread Group**).

3. Add a HTTP Request Sampler to the **Thread Group** by right-clicking on **Thread Group** and navigate to **Add | Sampler | HTTP Request**.

4. Under **HTTP Request**, change **Implementation** to **HttpClient4**.

5. Fill in the properties of the **HTTP Request Sampler** as follows:

   ○ **Server Name or IP**: `jmeterbook.aws.af.cm`

   ○ **Method**: `GET`

   ○ **Path**: `/person/list`

6. Add a Regular Expression Extractor as a child of the HTTP Request Sampler by right-clicking on **HTTP Request Sampler** and navigate to **Add | Post Processors | Regular Expression Extractor**.

7. Fill in the properties as follows:

   ○ **Reference Name**: `name`

   ○ **Regular Expression**: `"firstName":"(\w+?)",.+?,"lastName":"(\w+?)"`

   ○ **Template**: `$1$$2$`

   ○ **Match No**: `1`

   ○ **Default Value**: `name`

8. Add a Debug Sampler to the **Thread Group** by right-clicking on **Thread Group** and navigate to **Add | Sampler | Debug Sampler**.

9. Add a View Results Tree listener to the **Thread Group** by right-clicking on **Thread Group** and navigate to **Add | Listener | View Results Tree**.

10. Save the **Test Plan**.

The interesting bit here is the cryptic regular expression we are using here. It basically says to match words and store them in the variable defined as `name`. The `\w+?` regular expression instructs the pattern engine not to be greedy when matching and to stop on the first occurrence. The full capabilities of regular expressions are beyond the scope of this book, but we encourage you to master some as they will help you while scripting your scenarios. For now, just believe that it does what it says. Once you execute the test plan, you will be able to see the matches in the debug sampler of the View Results Tree. Here's a snippet of what you should expect to see:

```
name=firstName0lastName0
name_g=2
name_g0="firstName":"Larry","jobs":[{"id":1,"description":"Doctor"}],"
lastName":"Ellison"
name_g1=Larry
name_g2=Ellison
server=jmeterbook.aws.af.cm
```

Now let's shift gears to a more complicated example.

Using the BSF PostProcessor

When dealing with much more complicated JSON structures, you might find that the `Regular Expression Extractor` post processor just doesn't cut it. You might struggle to come up with the right regular expression to extract all the info you need. Examples of that might be deeply nested object graphs that have an embedded list of objects in them. At such times, a **BSF PostProcessor** will fit the bill. **BSF (Bean Scripting Framework)** is a set of Java classes that provide scripting language support within Java applications. This opens a whole realm of possibilities, allowing you to leverage the knowledge and power of scripting languages within your test plan while still retaining access to Java class libraries. Scripting languages supported within JMeter at the time of writing include AppleScript, JavaScript, BeanShell, ECMAScript, and Java to name a few. Let's jump right in with an example of querying Google's search service.

1. Launch JMeter.

2. Add a Thread Group to the **Test Plan** by right-clicking on **Test Plan** and navigate to **Add | Threads (Users) | Thread Group**.

3. Add a HTTP Request Sampler to the **Thread Group** by right-clicking on **Thread Group** and navigate to **Add | Sampler | HTTP Request**.

4. Under **HTTP Request**, change **Implementation** to **HttpClient4**.

5. Fill in the properties of the **HTTP Request Sampler** as follows:

   ○ **Server Name or IP**: `ajax.googleapis.com`

   ○ **Method**: `GET`

   ○ **Path**: `/ajax/services/search/web?v=1.0&q=Paris%20Hilton`

6. Add a BSF PostProcessor as a child of the **HTTP Request Sampler** by right-clicking on **HTTP Request Sampler** and navigate to **Add | Post Processors | BSF PostProcessor**:

   1. Pick JavaScript in the Language dropdown list

   2. In the **Scripts** text area, enter this:

      ```
      // Turn the JSON into an object called 'response'
      eval('var response = ' + prev.getResponseDataAsString());

      // Create a variable called haveBoots_# containing the
      number of matching URLs
      // For each result, create a variable called haveBoots and
      assign it the URL
      vars.put("url_cnt", response.responseData.results.length);

      //for each result, stop the URL as a JMeter variable
      for (var i = 0; i <= response.responseData.results.length;
      i++)
      {
        var x = response.responseData.results[i];
        vars.put("url_" + i, x.url);
      }
      ```

7. Add a Debug Sampler to the **Thread Group** by right-clicking on **Thread Group** and navigate to **Add | Sampler | Debug Sampler**.

8. Add a View Results Tree listener to the **Thread Group** by right-clicking on **Thread Group** and navigate to **Add | Listener | View Results Tree**.

9. Save the **Test Plan**.

Once saved, you can execute the test plan and see the full JSON returned by the request and the extracted values that have now been stored as JMeter variables. If all is correct, you should see values similar to the following:

```
url_0=http://www.parishilton.com/
url_1=http://en.wikipedia.org/wiki/Paris_Hilton
url_2=https://twitter.com/ParisHilton
url_3=http://www.imdb.com/name/nm0385296/
url_cnt=4
```

The BSF PostProcessor exposes a few variables that can be used in your scripts by default. In our preceding example, we have used two of them (`prev` and `var`). `prev` gives access to the previous sample result and `var` gives read/write access to variables. See a list of available variables at `http://jmeter.apache.org/usermanual/component_reference.html#BSF_PostProcessor`.

A quick run down of the code is as follows:

```
eval('var response = ' + prev.getResponseDataAsString());
```

Retrieves the response data of the previous sampler as a string and uses the JavaScript `eval()` function to turn it into a JSON structure. Take a look at the JavaDocs at `http://jmeter.apache.org/api/org/apache/jmeter/samplers/SampleResult.html` to see all the other methods available for the `prev` variable. Once a JSON structure has been extracted, we can call methods like we normally would in JavaScript.

```
vars.put("url_cnt", response.responseData.results.length);
```

This gets the size of the results that were returned and stores the result in a JMeter variable called `url_cnt`. The final bit of code iterates through the results and extracts the actual URLs and stores them into distinct JMeter variables `url_0` through `url_3`.

Handling the XML response

Yet another structure you may encounter as you build test plans is XML. Some websites may hand off XML as their response to certain calls. **XML (Extensible Markup Language)** allows you to describe object graphs in a different format than JSON does. For example, we could get our test application to return an XML representation of the person list we were working with earlier in this chapter by making a call to `http://jmeterbook.aws.af.cm/person/list?format=xml`. Describing XML in detail goes beyond the scope of this book, but you can find much more about it online. For our exercise, it will suffice just to know what it looks like. Have a look at the XML returned by the previous link.

Now that you know what XML looks like, let's get going with a sample test plan that deals with retrieving an XML response and extracting variables from it. Have a look at the XML we will be parsing at `http://search.maven.org/remotecontent?filepath=org/springframework/spring-test/3.2.1.RELEASE/spring-test-3.2.1.RELEASE.pom`. Our goal is to extract all the `artifactId` elements (deeply nested within the structure) into variables that we can then use later in our test plan, if we choose.

1. Launch JMeter.

2. Add a Thread Group to the **Test Plan** by right-clicking on **Test Plan** and navigate to **Add | Threads (Users) | Thread Group**.

3. Add a HTTP Request Sampler to the **Thread Group** by right-clicking on **Thread Group** and navigate to **Add | Sampler | HTTP Request**.

4. Under **HTTP Request**, change **Implementation** to HttpClient4.

5. Fill in the properties of the **HTTP Request Sampler** as follows:

    ○   **Server Name or IP**: `search.maven.org`

    ○   **Method**: `GET`

    ○   **Path**: `/remotecontent?filepath=org/springframework/spring-test/3.2.1.RELEASE/spring-test-3.2.1.RELEASE.pom`

6. Add a Save Responses to a file listener as a child of the **HTTP Request Sampler** by right-clicking on **HTTP Request Sampler** and navigate to **Add | Listener | Save Responses to a file**.

7. Fill in the properties of the **Save Responses** as follows:

    ○   **Filename prefix**: `xmlSample_`

    ○   **Variable name**: `testFile`

8. Add a XPath Extractor as a child of the **HTTP Request Sampler** by right-clicking on **HTTP Request Sampler** and navigate to **Add | Post Processors | XPath Extractor**.

9. Fill in the properties of the **HTTP Request Sampler** as follows:

    ○   **Reference name**: `artifact_id`

    ○   **XPath query**: `project/dependencies/dependency/artifactId`

    ○   **Default value**: `artifact_id`

10. Add a Debug Sampler to the **Thread Group** by right-clicking on **Thread Group | Add** and navigate to **Sampler | Debug Sampler**.

11. Add a View Results Tree listener to the **Thread Group** by right-clicking **Thread Group** and navigate to **Add** | **Listener** | **View Results Tree**.

12. Save the **Test Plan**.

Once saved, you will be able to execute the test plan and see the `artifact_id` variables in the View Results Tree listener. The only new element we have used here is the XPath Extractor post processor. This nifty JMeter component allows you to use the XPath query language to extract values from a structured XML or (X)HTML response. As such, we can extract an element deeply nested in the structure with this simple query: `project/dependencies/dependency/artifactId`.

This will look for the tail element (`artifactId`) of the query string within the following structure:

```
<project...>
  ...
  <dependencies>
    <dependency>
      <groupId>javax.activation</groupId>
      <artifactId>activation</artifactId>
      <version>1.1</version>
      <scope>provided</scope>
    </dependency>
    ...
  </dependencies>
</project>
```

This will return `activation`. That is exactly the information we are interested in. Now you know just how to get at the information you need when dealing with XML responses.

Summary

In this chapter, we have gone through the details of how to capture form submission in JMeter. We covered simple forms, with checkboxes and radio buttons. The same concepts covered in those sections can be applied to other input form elements such as text areas and comboboxes. We then explored how to deal with file uploads and downloads when recording test plans. Along the way, we addressed working with JSON data, both posting and consuming it. This exposed us to two powerful and flexible JMeter post processors, Regular Expression Extractor and BSF PostProcessor. Finally, we took a look at how to deal with XML data when we encounter it. For that, we covered yet another post processor JMeter offers, XPath Extractor PostProcessor. You should now be able to use what we have learned so far to accomplish most tasks you need to accomplish with forms while planning and scripting your test plans.

In the next chapter, we will dive into managing sessions with JMeter.

4
Managing Sessions

In this chapter, we'll cover session management in JMeter in detail. Web applications, by their very nature, use client and server sessions. Both work in harmony to give each user a distinct enclosure to maintain a series of communication with the server without affecting other users. For example, in *Chapter 2*, *Recording Your First Test*, the server session was created the moment a user logged in to the application, and maintained for all requests sent to the server by that user until he/she logged off or timed out. This is what protects other users from seeing each other's information. Depending on the application's architecture, the session may be maintained through cookies (most commonly used) or URL rewriting (less commonly used). The former maintains the session by sending a cookie in the HTTP headers of each request while the latter rewrites the URLs to append the session ID. The main differences are that the former relies on a client's browser choosing to accept cookies and is transparent to the application developer, while the latter isn't transparent and works regardless of if cookies are enabled or not. That said, diving into the details of the two modes goes beyond the scope of this book, but we would encourage you to spend some time reading some online resources to gain better understanding if you are the curious type. For this book, it will suffice to know that there are two modes and that JMeter handles both.

Let's dig right in and explore these scenarios and see how JMeter deals with each.

Managing sessions with cookies

A majority of web applications rely on cookies to maintain the session state. In the very early stages of the Internet, cookies were only used to keep the session ID. Things have since evolved and cookies now store a lot more information, such as user IDs and location preferences. The banking application we used as a case study in *Chapter 2, Recording Your First Test*, for example, relies on cookies to help each user maintain a valid session with the server, enabling the user to make a series of requests to the server. An example will help clear things up, so let's get right to one. For our example, some resources are protected based on the role of the user that is logged in. Users can have an admin or user role.

The steps to manage sessions with cookies are as follows:

1. Launch JMeter.
2. Start the HTTP proxy server (see *Chapter 2, Recording Your First Test*, if you don't know how).
3. In the browser, go to `http://jmeterbook.aws.af.cm/`.
4. Click on the **User Protected Resource** link (under **Chapter 4**).
5. Log in.
6. Fill in the **Username** field with `user1`.
7. Fill in the **Password** field with `password`.
8. Click on **Link** under **User resources**.
9. Log out.
10. Save the **Test Plan**.

Attempting to execute the recorded scenario upon saving it will not yield the expected results. Go ahead and add a **View Results Tree** listener (right-click on **Test Plan** and go to **Add | Listener | View Results Tree**) to diagnose what is actually going on. Once the simulation is run, examine the responses from the server through the **View Results Tree** listener. Even though all responses are green, indicating successful requests (since we got a response code of 200 from the server), we are actually still just getting back the login page after successfully logging in (see the **Response** tab of **View Results Tree** for subsequent requests after successful authentication).

If you examine the **Request** tab, you will see the reason for that. Following is a snippet of the `Request` data of the login process. You should see something similar to it:

```
GET
  http://jmeterbook.aws.af.cm/;jsessionid=2CE58BC032344AA90CA60C6C880
687A4

[no cookies]

Request Headers:
Connection: keep-alive
Content-Type: application/x-www-form-urlencoded
Accept-Language: en-US,en;q=0.8
Accept:
  text/html,application/xhtml+xml,application/xml;q=0.9,*/*;q=0.8
Origin: http://jmeterbook.aws.af.cm
User-Agent: Mozilla/5.0 (Macintosh; Intel Mac OS X 10_8_2)
  AppleWebKit/537.22 (KHTML, like Gecko) Chrome/25.0.1364.99
    Safari/537.22
Accept-Charset: ISO-8859-1,utf-8;q=0.7,*;q=0.3
Cache-Control: max-age=0
Referer: http://jmeterbook.aws.af.cm/login/auth
Accept-Encoding: gzip,deflate,sdch
Host: jmeterbook.aws.af.cm
```

Downloading the example code

You can download the example code files for all Packt books you have purchased from your account at http://www.packtpub.com. If you purchased this book elsewhere, you can visit http://www.packtpub.com/support and register to have the files e-mailed directly to you.

Notice two things here. First, there is a [no cookies] line present, indicating JMeter didn't find any stored cookie to use for this request. Second is the jsessionid cookie in the first line of the request. The server uses this to group all requests from a user under the same session ID, once authentication is established. If you compare this with the subsequent calls in **View Results Tree**, you will notice different jsessionid values, further indicating that the server is treating those subsequent calls as new requests and not associating it with a previous request. Thirdly, the URL for subsequent calls also mimics what we saw earlier in http://jmeterbook.aws.af.cm/login/auth, indicating that we are actually being asked to authenticate again on the login page since the server didn't associate our requests for protected resources with the same jsessionid cookie.

```
GET
  http://jmeterbook.aws.af.cm/login/auth;jsessionid=0B478A8A1F93D68D14
745261D0A7E792

[no cookies]
...
```

All this is evidence that JMeter is not currently managing the session appropriately. But how can it? We have not instructed it to. JMeter comes with a couple of components to help maintain sessions. Since our sample here relies on cookies to maintain sessions, we will use the **HTTP Cookie Manager** component. This component stores and sends cookies just as web browsers do. If an HTTP request and response contains a cookie, the Cookie Manager automatically stores that cookie and will use it for all future requests to the application.

> Since a thread is synonymous to a user in JMeter, each thread has its own cookie storage area, giving us the ability to run multiple users for a simulation with each maintaining a separate session.

This is exactly what we want. Let's go ahead and add a Cookie Manager to our test plan. Right-click on **Test Plan** and navigate to **Test Plan | Add | Config Element | HTTP Cookie Manager** (see the upcoming screenshot). This component allows you to define additional cookies, but the default will usually suffice except in cases where your application might be doing something tricky. Once that is added, if we rerun our test plan and examine the **Request** tab, we will see a different outcome. This time, the jsessionid cookie is stored and maintained across requests and the [no cookie] line is gone. Here is a snippet of the two subsequent requests in **View Results Tree**:

```
GET http://jmeterbook.aws.af.cm/login/auth

Cookie Data:
JSESSIONID=013FA93C2AABB31EBE8FDF8CCC575F09
GET http://jmeterbook.aws.af.cm/secure/user

Cookie Data:
JSESSIONID=013FA93C2AABB31EBE8FDF8CCC575F09
```

Notice that the same session ID is maintained across the requests. If you examine the `Response` data, you will see that we are now able to access the intended protected resources. Refer to the following screenshot, which shows how to use the **HTTP Cookie Manager** component to define additional cookies:

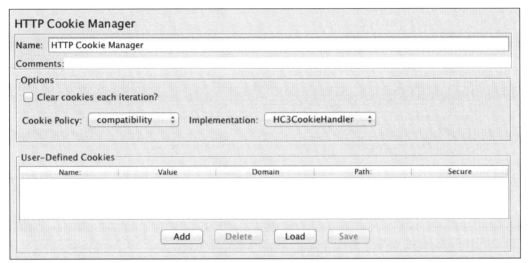

The HTTP Cookie Manager

This completes our exploration of the **HTTP Cookie Manager** element. It is possible to have more than one Cookie Manager in a test plan depending on the application needs. For example, if you have multiple thread groups within a test plan, it is possible to have a Cookie Manager per thread group.

> If there is more than one Cookie Manager in the scope of a sampler, there is no way to specify which will be used. Also, a cookie stored in one Cookie Manager is not available to any other manager, so exercise caution when using multiple Cookie Managers.

Managing sessions with URL rewriting

In the absence of cookie support, the alternative method web applications use to manage session information is a technique known as URL rewriting. With this approach, the session ID is attached to all URLs that are within the HTML page that is sent as a response to the client. This ensures that the session ID is automatically sent back to the server as part of the request, without the need to put it in the header. The advantage of this technique is that it works even if a client browser has cookies disabled. Let's examine a sample and see how JMeter comes to the rescue.

1. Launch JMeter.
2. Start the **HTTP Proxy Server** (see *Chapter 2, Recording Your First Test*, if you don't know how).
3. In the browser, go to `http://jmeterbook.aws.af.cm`.
4. Click on the **URL Rewrite Sample link** under **Chapter 4**.
5. Click on **First Link**.
6. Click on **Another Link** (at the bottom of the page).
7. Click on the **Home** link.
8. Click on **Second Link**.
9. Click on the **jmeter-book** link on the banner on the navigation bar at the top.
10. Save the **Test Plan**.

If you re-execute the test plan after saving it, you'll notice that all the links have a `jsessionid` cookie appended to them. This ensures that the same session ID is sent along to the server, thereby treating our series of request as one whole conversation with the server; in short, our session is maintained. Since we recorded this, the session ID sent with all the requested links is the one the server generated at the time we recorded. Obviously, we will need to turn this into a variable that can then be used for multiple threads, as each new thread will be treated as a new user with each getting their own unique session ID.

To do that, we'll employ JMeter's **HTTP URL Re-writing Modifier** component. This component is similar to the **HTML Link Parser** modifier except that its specific purpose is to extract session IDs from the response; that is, a page or link. Let's add this to the test plan (right-click on **Thread Group** and navigate to **Thread Group | Pre Processors | HTTP URL Re-writing Modifier**). See the following screenshot to see what the configuration elements are. The most important parameter there is **Session Argument Name**. This allows you to specify the session ID parameter name to grab from the response. This may vary based on your application. Java web applications, for example, usually have this as jsessionid (as in our case) or JSESSIONID. Web applications that are not written in Java might have a variation of this; for example, SESSION_ID. Inspect the application under test and see what key the session ID is getting stored in. That value is what goes into this parameter box. In our case, it is simply jsessionid. Refer to the following screenshot to see the configuration elements of the **HTTP URL Re-writing Modifier**:

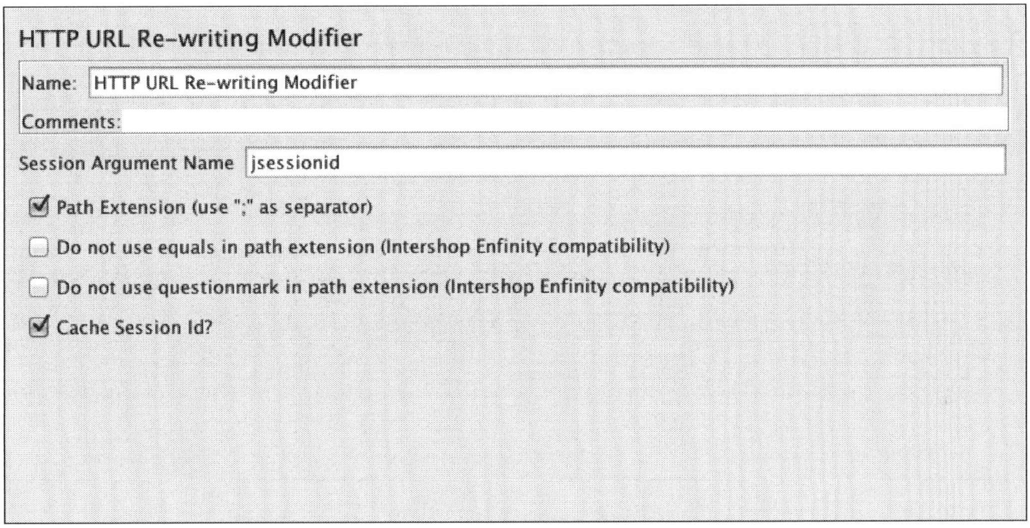

The HTTP URL Re-writing Modifier

The other options that can be configured are:

- **Path Extension**: If checked, a semicolon will be used to separate the session ID and the argument URL. Java web applications fall into this category, so go ahead and check it for our sample.

- **Do not use equals in path extension**: If checked, omits the use of = when capturing the rewrite URL. Java web applications use =, so we leave this unchecked.

- **Do not use questionmark in path extension**: This prevents the query string from ending up in the path extension. We will leave it unchecked.

- **Cache Session Id**: Saves the value of the session ID for later use, when it is not present, for example, in subsequent page requests. We check this option as it applies to us. We want the same session ID sent for all page requests by a thread/user.

The last thing to clean up before we rerun our test plan is the already existing session IDs that were captured during our recording. Go through each sampler and delete that from the URL request paths. So, for example, this:

```
/urlRewrite/link1;jsessionid=9074385741E66F07B36286763FF8C2FD
```

Should become the following:

```
/urlRewrite/link1
```

This will be captured by the **HTTP URL Re-writing Modifier** component and appended to subsequent calls automatically. At this point, we are ready to rerun our sample and see the outcome. Remember to add a **View Results Tree** listener to the plan if you haven't already done so. Once run, we should be able to verify that the outcome is what we expected. The same session ID should be maintained for subsequent requests from a user. Below is a snippet of three subsequent requests from the same thread, all maintaining the same session ID (**774F9D6220F76C54CA346D0365A33998**).

```
GET
  http://jmeterbook.aws.af.cm/urlRewrite/index;jsessionid=774F9D6220F7
6C54CA346D0365A33998

[no cookies]

Request Headers:
Connection: keep-alive
```

```
Accept-Language: en-US,en;q=0.5
Accept: text/html,application/xhtml+xml,application/
xml;q=0.9,*/*;q=0.8
User-Agent: Mozilla/5.0 (Macintosh; Intel Mac OS X 10.8; rv:16.0)
  Gecko/20100101 Firefox/16.0
Referer: http://jmeterbook.aws.af.cm/
Accept-Encoding: gzip, deflate
Host: jmeterbook.aws.af.cm

GET
  http://jmeterbook.aws.af.cm/urlRewrite/link1;jsessionid=774F9D6220F7
6C54CA346D0365A33998

GET
  http://jmeterbook.aws.af.cm/urlRewrite/link3;jsessionid=774F9D6220F7
6C54CA346D0365A33998
```

Although we have placed the element at the Thread Group level, it can also be placed at the sampler level. In such a case, it will modify only that request and not affect subsequent calls. You may need such flexibility in some situations.

This wraps up the different ways in which we can manage sessions with JMeter. The web applications you test will normally fall under one of these two major categories, cookie management or URL rewriting. Based on your needs, JMeter provides components to help manage sessions for both.

Summary

In this chapter, we have covered how JMeter helps manage web sessions for your test plans. First we examined the most common way web applications manage sessions, using a cookie. For these cases, JMeter provides a component called **HTTP Cookie Manager**, whose primary job is to help capture the cookie generated by the server and store it for future use during test execution. We then explored web applications that use URL rewriting to maintain sessions as opposed to cookies. This led us to the **HTTP URL Re-writing Modifier**, another component JMeter provides for handling these cases.

In conclusion, what we have covered here should suffice in helping you effectively manage sessions as you build test plans for your own applications.

In the next chapter, we will cover resource monitoring.

5
Resource Monitoring

So far, we have seen how JMeter can help with conducting performance testing. In this chapter, we will explore what it offers in terms of resource monitoring. Resource monitoring is a broad subject that covers analyzing system hardware usage, which includes CPU, memory, disk, and network. As you conduct testing, it is important to know how each of these resources are behaving under load to better understand if there are bottlenecks and address them accordingly. Most organizations have dedicated teams (for example, network and system engineers) for configuring and monitoring these resources. In addition, there are dedicated tools for monitoring and analyzing them. Tools such as HP OpenView, CA Wily Introscope (now CA Application Performance Management), New Relic, and profiler agent probes were created for this very purpose. We have said all that to say that what JMeter offers pales in comparison to what you will get using such dedicated tools. Moreover, not all companies can afford such tools or have personnel in charge of setting up adequate monitoring. You just might be a one-man shop doing testing and monitoring all by yourself!

Since this is a book on JMeter, let's see how we can go about doing some resource monitoring with it.

Basic server monitoring

JMeter comes with an out-of-the-box monitoring controller. This allows you to monitor the general health of the application or web server. These include light-weight web containers such as Jetty, Apache Tomcat, Resin, or fully-stacked, heavier ones such as WebSphere, Weblogic, JBoss, Geronimo, and Oracle OCJ4. Metrics such as active threads, memory, health, and load are gathered and reported in a graphical form. Having such metrics makes it easier to see the relationship between server performance and response time on the clients. Multiple servers can be monitored using a single monitor controller. Although originally designed to work with the Apache Tomcat server (`http://tomcat.apache.org/`), any servlet container (`http://en.wikipedia.org/wiki/Servlet_container`) supporting **JMX (Java Management Extension)** can port the Tomcat status servlet to provide the same information. Providing such ports for other servers goes beyond the scope of this book, so we will stick to using Apache Tomcat for our use case.

Monitoring servers during test executions helps identify potential bottlenecks in the application or system resources. It can draw focus to long-running queries, insufficient thread and data source pools, insufficient heap size, high I/O activity, server capacity inadequacies, slow-performing application components, CPU usage, and so on. All these are important to troubleshooting performance issues and attaining the targeted goals.

To get started, we first need a server to monitor. Let's download Apache Tomcat and get it up and running.

Setting up Apache Tomcat Server

1. Download Apache Tomcat from `http://tomcat.apache.org/download-70.cgi`. At the time of writing, version 7.0.37 was the latest. That is what we will use for our purposes, though an older version should work just as well.

2. Get the ZIP or compressed TAR file.

3. Extract the contents of the archive to a location of your choosing. We will refer to this as TOMCAT_HOME for the remainder of this chapter.

4. From the command line, switch to the TOMCAT_HOME/bin directory

5. Start the server to verify that the installation was successful

   ○ On Windows, run the following:

   ```
   catalina.bat run
   ```

   ○ On Unix, run this:

   ```
   ./catalina.sh run
   ```

If all goes OK, the server should start up and you should see something similar to the following on the console:

```
Mar 16, 2013 8:55:12 AM org.apache.coyote.AbstractProtocol init
INFO: Initializing ProtocolHandler ["http-bio-8080"]
Mar 16, 2013 8:55:12 AM org.apache.coyote.AbstractProtocol init
INFO: Initializing ProtocolHandler ["ajp-bio-8009"]
Mar 16, 2013 8:55:12 AM org.apache.catalina.startup.Catalina load
INFO: Initialization processed in 1282 ms
Mar 16, 2013 8:55:13 AM org.apache.catalina.core.StandardService
startInternal
INFO: Starting service Catalina
Mar 16, 2013 8:55:13 AM org.apache.catalina.core.StandardEngine
startInternal
INFO: Starting Servlet Engine: Apache Tomcat/7.0.37
...
INFO: Deploying web application directory /Users/berinle/devtools/server/
apache-tomcat-7.0.37/webapps/ROOT
Mar 16, 2013 8:55:13 AM org.apache.coyote.AbstractProtocol start
INFO: Starting ProtocolHandler ["http-bio-8080"]
Mar 16, 2013 8:55:13 AM org.apache.coyote.AbstractProtocol start
INFO: Starting ProtocolHandler ["ajp-bio-8009"]
Mar 16, 2013 8:55:13 AM org.apache.catalina.startup.Catalina start
INFO: Server startup in 981 ms
```

If the server doesn't start up, it could be that JAVA_HOME is not properly set (see *Chapter 1, Performance Testing Fundamentals*, for details) or the executable files in the bin directory don't have the right permissions. Please refer to the Apache Tomcat documentation for more details, at http://tomcat.apache.org/tomcat-7.0-doc/setup.html.

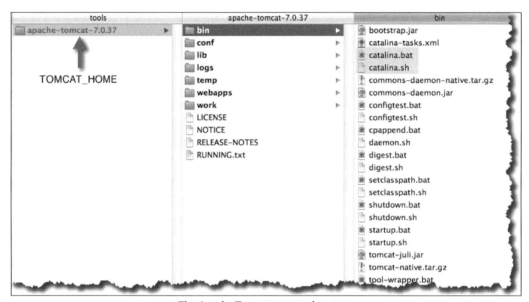

The Apache Tomcat extracted content

Go to `http://localhost:8080` and verify that you are greeted with the Apache Tomcat home screen.

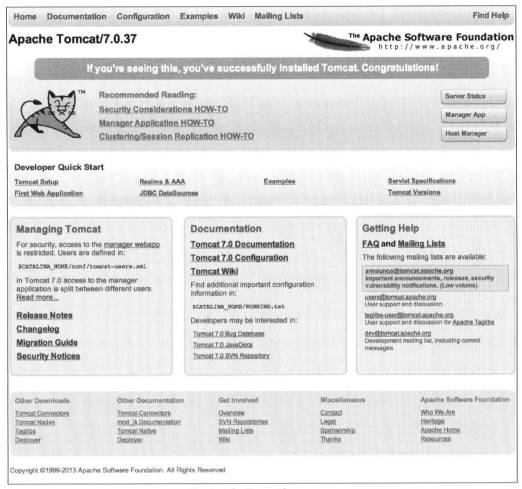

The Apache Tomcat home screen

Congratulations, your server is now up and running! To monitor it, we need to perform one more step on the server. We need to set up at least one user account with the proper role on the server to get us the information we need. The account we set up will later be used when we configure the monitoring controller in JMeter.

Configuring Tomcat users

The following are the steps to configure Tomcat users:

1. Navigate to `TOMCAT_HOME/conf`.

2. Open `tomcat-users.xml` in any suitable editor.

3. Between `<tomcat-users>` and `</tomcat-users>`, add the following:

   ```
   <role rolename="manager-gui"/>
   <user username="admin" password="admin" roles="manager-gui"/>
   ```

   This creates a user named `admin` with password `admin` for authenticating with the Tomcat manager application.

4. Save the file.

5. Restart your server by stopping it (*Ctrl + C*) from the console you started it from earlier and starting it again to make sure the configuration changes are picked up.

6. Navigate to `http://localhost:8080/manager/html`.

7. Enter the login credentials (`admin` for both username and password) when prompted.

8. You should now be able to see the **manager** page as shown in the following screenshot.

Finally, with the server configuration behind us, we can now proceed with setting up JMeter to monitor the server.

The contents of `tomcat-users.xml` are as follows:

```
<?xml version='1.0' encoding='utf-8'?>
<tomcat-users>
  <role rolename="manager-gui"/>
  <user username="admin" password="admin" roles="manager-gui"/>
</tomcat-users>
```

Authenticating with Tomcat Application Manager

Setting up a monitor controller in JMeter

The following are the steps to set up a monitor controller in JMeter:

1. Launch JMeter.

2. Add a new Thread Group by navigating to **Test Plan | Add | Threads (Users) | Thread Group**.

3. Add an HTTP Authorization Manager by navigating to **Thread Group | Add | Config Element | HTTP Authorization Manager**.

   ° **Base URL**: (leave blank)

   ° **Username**: admin

   ° **Password**: admin

   ° **Domain**: (leave blank)

   ° **Realm**: (leave blank)

4. Add an HTTP Request by navigating to **Thread Group | Add | Sampler | HTTP Request**.

   ° **Name**: Server Status (optional)

   ° **Server Name**: localhost

   ° **Port Number**: 8080

   ° **Path**: /manager/status

5. Add a request parameter named XML, in uppercase. Give it a value of `true` (in lowercase).

6. Check **User Monitor** at the bottom of the sampler.

7. Add a constant timer with a thread delay of `5000` milliseconds by navigating to **Thread Group | Add | Timer | Constant Timer**.

8. Add a Monitor listener by navigating to **Thread Group | Add | Listener | Monitor Results**.

9. Save the **Test Plan**.

10. Now we have JMeter all set up and ready to monitor the server. We could go ahead and execute the test plan now, but we won't see too much in terms of results, since there is no activity on the server and we need to have JMeter actively monitoring during such activities. We have prepared a test plan using examples that came with Apache Tomcat (`basic-monitor-sampler.jmx`), so grab it and let's use that to put some load on the server. Assuming you haven't changed the default server ports of Tomcat, the provided test plan should work right off the bat.

11. Before starting the provided test plan, let's change the monitor test plan to loop forever, so we can watch the server metrics as activity continues on the server.

12. For the monitor test plan, click on **Thread Group** and check the **forever** box for the loop count. Save the test plan.

For the constant timer in the monitor test plan, intervals shorter than 5 seconds add stress to the server. You should consult with infrastructure engineers in your company (if any) to see what an acceptable interval might be before configuring monitoring for a production environment. As a rule of thumb, 5 seconds is a decent number.

To run the provided test plan alongside the monitoring test plan, you need to launch another instance of JMeter and open the provided test plan in it.

So, without further ado, let's kick off the monitor test plan and then execute the provided test plan to put stress on the server and see the monitoring results. If it has all been set up properly, you should see some results starting to show up under the monitor results listener. The **Health** tab might look similar to the following screenshot, and the **Performance** tab like the screenshot after that. As you can see from the following screenshot, our run gradually progressed from healthy and stopped at active at the end of the simulation run. We didn't get to warning or dead levels, which is a good sign our server stayed healthy overall.

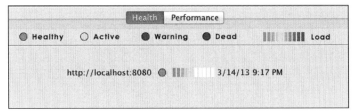

The Monitor Results listener (Health tab)

In the following screenshot, you can see the memory (represented by the yellow line) and load (represented by the blue line) gradually spike up during our simulation. The thread percentage (represented by the red line) and health (represented by the green line) also stayed at healthy levels, consistent with what we observed.

That wraps up our look into basic monitoring with JMeter. In the next section, we will see how we can leverage JMeter's plugin architecture and use a plugin to provide even more granular monitoring metrics for our needs.

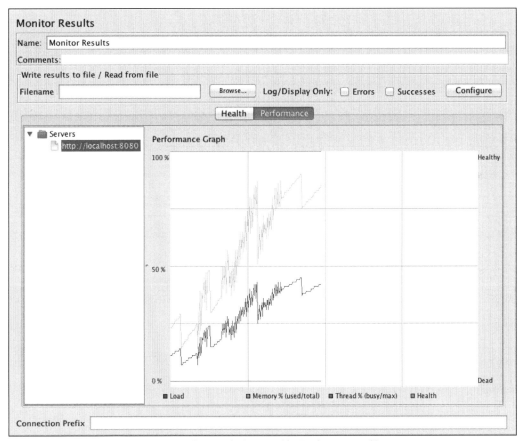

Monitor the Results listener (the Performance tab)

Monitoring the server with a JMeter plugin

So far we have examined how we can use the inbuilt server monitoring capabilities of JMeter to monitor server health. While this might be OK for basic needs, it falls short for advanced needs. For instance, the graphs generated don't provide CPU and disk I/O metrics that could be deemed critical for your analysis. To get such metrics, you could extend JMeter with a suite of plugins that give better results. JMeter plugins, hosted on Google code at `https://code.google.com/p/jmeter -plugins/`, is a neat project that aims to extend JMeter with some much-needed features that are lacking out of the box. The project provides additional samplers, graphs, listeners, and so on, all of which make it easier to work with JMeter. In this section, we will install this suite of plugins and use the monitoring capability it provides to get better metrics.

The only prerequisite for installing it is that you are running JMeter 2.8 or later with JRE (the Java Runtime Environment) 1.6 or higher.

Installing the plugins

The plugin comes with three archives, all of which must be extracted to different destinations. At the time of writing, the project was at version 1.0.0, which is what we will be working with.

1. Download `JMeterPlugins-1.0.0.zip`. This archive contains JMeter custom plugins.

2. Download `JMeterPlugins-libs-1.0.0.zip`. This archive contains additional third party JARs used by some of the custom plugins provided.

3. Download `ServerAgent-1.0.0.zip`. This archive contains server resource monitoring agents to use with the PerfMon Metrics Collector plugin standalone utility.

4. Extract the contents of `JMeterPlugins-1.0.0.zip` into `JMETER_HOME/lib/ext`.

5. Extract the contents of `JMeterPlugins-libs-1.0.0.zip` into `JMETER_HOME/lib`.

6. Extract the contents of `ServerAgent-1.0.0.zip` into `TOMCAT_HOME`.

With those steps, we have installed a whole suite of plugins, adding new features to JMeter. If you were to relaunch JMeter now, you will notice additional samplers, listeners, timers, and so on, all beginning with `jp@gc` to distinguish them from the bundled ones.

Let's start the server agent, which will feed the JMeter listener probe we will add to our test plan later.

1. Start a shell or DOS prompt.

2. Navigate to `TOMCAT_HOME\serveragent`.

3. Start the agent.

    ° On Windows, run the following:

       startAgent.bat

    ° On Unix, run this:

       ./startAgent.sh

You should get logs similar to the following ones if the agent has started successfully:

```
INFO    2013-03-16 19:13:33.328 [kg.apc.p] (): Binding UDP to 4444
INFO    2013-03-16 19:13:34.329 [kg.apc.p] (): Binding TCP to 4444
INFO    2013-03-16 19:13:34.334 [kg.apc.p] (): JP@GC Agent v2.2.0 started
```

As you can see, the agent has started on port `4444`, the default. We will use this port later when configuring the monitor listener for JMeter. If this port is not satisfactory for you, the plugin provides configuration files that can be edited to choose a desired port. Please refer to the documentation at `https://code.google.com/p/jmeter-plugins/`.

With the server agent running, let's add a few monitor listeners to our test plan. For our purposes, we have chosen the sample test plan we recorded using the samples provided by Apache Tomcat.

 Please note that this same concept can be applied to other applications deployed on the same server where the monitor agent has been installed.

Adding monitor listeners to the test plan

1. Launch JMeter.

2. Open the provided test plan (`advanced-monitoring-sampler-1.jmx`).

3. Add a PerfMon Metrics Collector listener byright-clicking on **Test Plan** and navigating to **Test Plan | Add | Listener | jp@gc – PerfMon Metrics Collector**.

   ○ Add one row each to gather these metrics (`CPU`, `Memory`, `Network I/O`, and `Disks I/O`)

   ○ **Host / IP**: `localhost`

   ○ **Port**: `4444`

   ○ **Metrics to collect** (dropdown): **CPU**, **Memory**, **Network I/O**, and **Disks I/O**

4. Add a Response Times vs Threads listener by right-clicking on **Test Plan** and navigating to **Test Plan | Add | Listener | jp@gc – Response Times vs Threads**.

5. Add a Transactions per Second listener by right-clicking on **Test Plan** and navigating to **Test Plan | Add | Listener | jp@gc – Transactions per Second**.

6. Save the **Test Plan**.

With the server agent running, and our additional monitor listeners set up, we are ready to kick off the simulation execution. Let's go right on and execute it. While it's executing, you can see the graphical representation of the metrics you have chosen to analyze if you click on **jp@gc - PerfMon Metrics Collector**. As you can see from the following screenshot, CPU is spiking up and down, showing quite a decent load on the server. Memory stays almost constant while network, which is relatively stable, spiked quite high two minutes into our simulation run. It immediately dropped down, back to the low ranges after the spike, so something might have transpired on the network at the time of the execution run, causing such a spike. Since this test plan doesn't involve any disk I/O, it stays on 0 for the duration of our simulation.

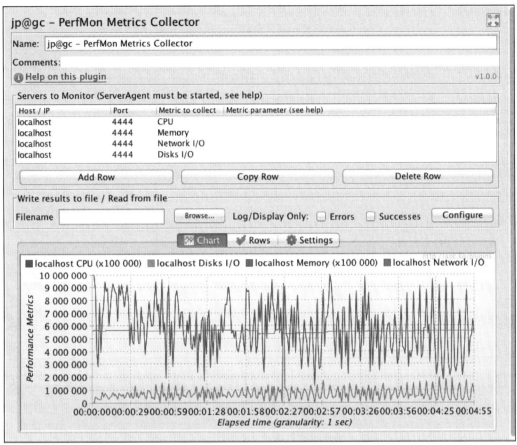

The PerfMon Metrics Collector

The **Response Time vs. Threads** listener shows a true picture of how much time the server takes to service each request in relation to the number of executing threads. The graph can be a bit messy to read, so in the **Rows** tab, you can check only the requests you are interested in analyzing. We have done just that in the following screenshot, and chose only a handful of requests. As you can see, we have a maximum number of 20 threads running, and the highest response time from this graph was for the `/examples/jsp/chat` request, when about 13 threads were running.

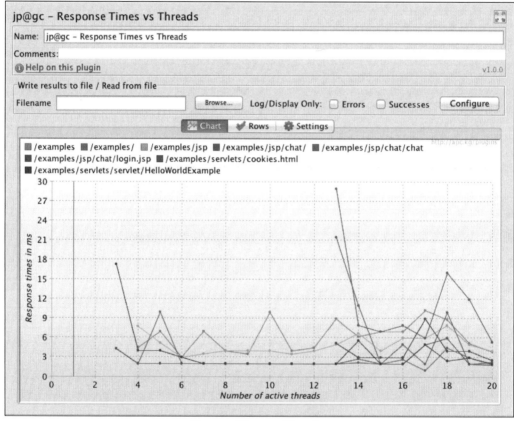

Response Times vs. Threads

Though the graph isn't shown here, the last listener we added was the Transactions per Second listener. It shows just how many requests (transactions) the server was able to handle during the course of our simulation run on a second-by-second basis. Like the **Response Times vs Threads** listener, the chart can be messy and you will need to selectively choose which requests you were interested in to make some sense of the graph.

As you can see, these new listeners, along with the server agent, allow you to monitor resources in far greater detail than with those shipped with JMeter. In addition to the metrics we gathered, you can choose to gather additional ones including swap, TCP, and JMX if those were areas of concern. By and large, we can use this to effectively monitor resources on the server.

 Although we have only set this up for one server, the monitor can be set up to monitor multiple servers; for example, in cases where you have a cluster of servers.

Summary

In this chapter, we walked through how JMeter can help with monitoring server resources. To do that, we set up an Apache Tomcat server. Once done, we examined the built-in capabilities of JMeter with regards to monitoring. We further examined how we could get more granular monitoring metrics by extending JMeter with custom-developed plugins. This allowed us to monitor server resources such as CPU, disk I/O, memory, and network I/O, among other things. Through the plugin, we also got additional samplers, timers, processors, and listeners that allowed us to monitor transactions per second and response time versus thread metrics. Though not an extensive monitoring tool, JMeter proved itself a capable tool to do basic monitoring of server resources.

In the next chapter, we will go into depth on distributed testing and see how to leverage the capabilities of JMeter to accomplish this.

6

Distributed Testing

There will come a time when running your test plans on a single machine won't cut it any longer performance-wise, since resources on the single box are limited. For example, this could be the case when you want to spin-off a thousand users for a test plan. Depending on the power and resources of the machine you are testing on, and the nature of your test plans, a single machine can probably spin-off with 300-600 threads before starting to error out or causing inaccurate test results. There are several reasons why this may happen. One is because there is a limit to the amount of threads you can spin-off on a single machine. Most operating systems guard against complete system failure by placing such limits on hosted applications. Also, your use case may require you to simulate requests from various IP addresses. Distributed testing allows you to replicate tests across many low-end machines, enabling you to start more threads and thereby simulating more load on the server. In this chapter, we will learn how to leverage JMeter for distributed testing and put more load on the server under test in the process.

Remote testing with JMeter

JMeter has inbuilt support for distributed testing. This enables a single JMeter GUI instance, known as the **master**, to control a number of remote JMeter instances, known as **slaves**, and collect all the test results from them. The features offered by this approach include:

- Saving test samples to the local machine
- Managing multiple instances of **JMeterEngine** (slave nodes) from a single machine
- Replicating the test plan from the master node to each controlled server without the need to copy them to each server

JMeter does not distribute the load between servers.
Each server will execute the same test plan in its entirety.

Though the test plan is replicated across to each server, the data needed by the test plan, if any, is not. In cases where input data such as CSV data is needed to run the tests, such data needs to be made available on each server where the test plan will be executed.

 The remote mode is more resource intensive than running the same number of non-GUI tests independently. If many server instances are used, the client's JMeter can become overloaded, as can the client's network connection.

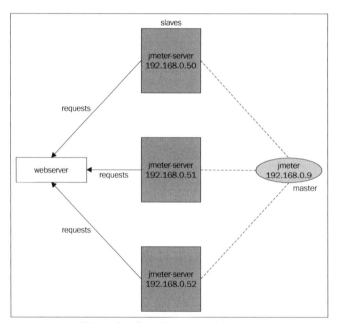

JMeter distributed testing architecture

 It is important for all slave nodes and the master node to run the same version of JMeter, and if possible the same version of the Java Runtime Environment. Mostly, minor JRE variations are fine, but not major ones. For example, it is okay for the master to be running on JRE 1.6.12 and slaves on 1.6.17, but 1.6.xx with 1.5.xx is not.

Configuring JMeter slave nodes

There are a number of ways to get the slave nodes going. In this section, we will go over two options that will often fit the bill for accomplishing your goals.

The most obvious is to go out and buy new machines just for this purpose. For most of us, that is not feasible. Another option is to get hold of extra computers lying around in the office, configure them appropriately, and use them for this purpose. While that will work perfectly, it might be time-consuming to get all of the boxes set up without the appropriate tools, knowledge, and expertise. Yet another option is to use virtual machines to accomplish the same outcome. This is the option we will be focusing on in this section. We favor this approach for the following reasons:

- We don't necessarily need another physical machine to try out distributed testing

- We can leverage **Vagrant** and **Puppet**, excellent infrastructure automation tools, to set up virtual boxes with the required software with little interaction from us

- We can be up and running with a few virtual machines in less time than it takes to run to your local coffee shop and grab a cup of coffee

- It is free

- The same concepts can be applied to leverage machines in the cloud (AWS, Rackspace, and so on) to test

In case you haven't heard of Vagrant before, don't be alarmed. It's an excellent tool that makes building development environments easy. It allows you to create and configure lightweight, reproducible, and portable development environments. Elaborating on the uses of Vagrant and Puppet go beyond the scope of this book, but I would encourage you to read more about them at `http://www.vagrantup.com` and `https://puppetlabs.com/`. Grab a copy of Vagrant at `http://downloads.vagrantup.com/`. At the time of writing, version 1.1.4 was the latest and that is what we will be using in this chapter.

For the book, We have prepared the necessary scripts needed to provision boxes. The only requirement to use the scripts is to have Oracle's **VirtualBox** installed on your machine. VirtualBox comes with installers for Windows, Mac OS, Solaris, and Linux. You can grab a copy of the operating system of your choice at `https://www.virtualbox.org/wiki/Downloads`. At the time of writing, VirtualBox was at Version 4.2.10 and that is what we have installed.

With both Vagrant and VirtualBox installed, we are ready to configure our distributed testing environment. Let's go right ahead and do that.

Configuring one slave per machine

In this configuration, we are going to set up three slave machines and control them with one master client. This will mimic having four separate physical machines with one of them acting as master (where the JMeter GUI client runs) and the other three acting as slave nodes (where the JMeter server scripts are kicked-off).

1. Download the Vagrant project provided for this section (978-1-78216-584-2_6_1_codes.zip).

2. Extract the contents to a folder named node_one.

3. On the command line, go to the node_one folder.

4. Run **Vagrant** by typing vagrant up.

5. Choose the appropriate connection to bridge. For example, if you are on a wireless connection, choose **en1: Wi-Fi**. If you are on Ethernet, choose **en0: Ethernet**.

In a few moments, a fully functional VirtualBox will be created with JMeter installed and ready to run! You should see logs similar to the following:

```
[default] Running provisioner: VagrantPlugins::Puppet::Provisioner::Puppet...
Running Puppet with main.pp...
stdin: is not a tty
warning: Could not retrieve fact fqdn
notice: /Stage[main]//Package[curl]/ensure: ensure changed 'purged' to 'present'
notice: /Stage[main]//Exec[download_jmeter]/returns: executed successfully
notice: /Stage[main]//Package[git-core]/ensure: ensure changed 'purged' to 'present'
notice: /Stage[main]//Package[zsh]/ensure: ensure changed 'purged' to 'present'
notice: /Stage[main]//Package[vim]/ensure: ensure changed 'purged' to 'present'
notice: /Stage[main]/Java::Package_debian/Package[java]/ensure: ensure changed 'purged' to 'present'
notice: Finished catalog run in 56.75 seconds
```

Don't take our word for it though; verify that the box is properly configured by performing the following on the command line (from the node_one folder):

```
vagrant ssh
```

```
cd apache-jmeter-2.9/bin
./jmeter --version
```

This should show you the version of JMeter that you are running on the guest machine. In my case, as you can see in the following log, it reports `Version 2.9 r1437961`:

```
vagrant ssh
Welcome to Ubuntu 12.04 LTS (GNU/Linux 3.2.0-23-generic-pae i686)


 * Documentation:  https://help.ubuntu.com/
Welcome to your Vagrant-built virtual machine.
Last login: Fri Sep 14 06:22:31 2012 from 10.0.2.2
vagrant@precise32:~$ cd apache-jmeter-2.9/bin
vagrant@precise32:~/apache-jmeter-2.9/bin$ ./jmeter --version
Copyright (c) 1998-2013 The Apache Software Foundation
Version 2.9 r1437961
```

If we attempt to kick off the JMeter server on this node now (from the `apache-jmeter-2.9/bin` directory, run `./jmeter-server`), we will encounter an error like the following:

```
vagrant@precise32:~/apache-jmeter-2.9/bin$ ./jmeter-server

Created remote object: UnicastServerRef [liveRef:
[endpoint:[127.0.1.1:43765](local),objID:[67bbc70b:13da4550a5f:-7fff,
-2865662902309525657]]]
Server failed to start: java.rmi.RemoteException: Cannot start. precise32
is a loopback address.
An error occurred: Cannot start. precise32 is a loopback address.
```

This is because the server is returning an IP address of `127.0.1.1`, which is considered a loop back address. To fix that, we need to find out the assigned IP address of the virtual machine and edit `apache-jmeter-2.9/bin/jmeter-server` to add that IP address. To get the assigned IP address from the newly created virtual machine, run this on the command line:

```
ifconfig | grepinet
```

The line of interest here is the line containing 192.168.x.x. For our node, the assigned IP address is `192.168.1.27`.

```
inet addr:10.0.2.15  Bcast:10.0.2.255  Mask:255.255.255.0
inet6addr: fe80::a00:27ff:fe12:9698/64 Scope:Link
```

```
inet addr:192.168.1.27  Bcast:192.168.1.255  Mask:255.255.255.0
inet6addr: fe80::a00:27ff:fe66:422c/64 Scope:Link
inet addr:127.0.0.1  Mask:255.0.0.0
         inet6 addr: ::1/128 Scope:Host
```

Now edit `apache-jmeter-2.9/bin/jmeter-server` using the command `vi apache-jmeter-2.9/bin/jmeter-server`. Look for the line beginning with `RMI_HOST_DEF` and add the following just below it:

`RMI_HOST_DEF=-Djava.rmi.server.hostname=192.168.1.27`

> Be sure to replace `192.168.1.27` with the assigned IP address of your own virtual box.

Save the file (by pressing *Esc* and then typing `:wq`) and this machine is ready to act as a server. Before we configure a second node, it would be wise to take the first for a spin. Let's run `JMETER_HOME/bin/jmeter-server` on the machine once again. This time it should succeed and you should see something similar to the following on the console:

```
Created remote object: UnicastServerRef [liveRef:
[endpoint:[192.168.1.27:46313](local),objID:[62a8e304:13da47c073a:-7fff,
-369620866826328728]]]
```

Now it is waiting for instructions from the master. Let's go right ahead and configure the master to control it.

Configuring the master node to be tested against one slave per machine

Now that we have one slave node configured, we can test it out by configuring the master node to connect to it and control it. To do that, we will have to add the slave node's IP address to the master's node configuration file.

On the host machine (where the JMeter GUI client is running), perform the following steps:

1. Open `JMETER_HOME/bin/jmeter.properties`.
2. Look for the line beginning with `remote_hosts=127.0.0.1`.
3. Change it to `remote_hosts=192.168.1.27`.

4. `192.168.1.27` should be changed to match the assigned IP address of your virtual box.

5. Save the file.

6. Launch JMeter.

7. Navigate to **Run | Remote Start | Slave IP address**, where **Slave IP address** is the assigned IP address of your virtual machine.

By clicking on the **Slave IP address**, the master node will make a connection with the remote server running on the VirtualBox. You should see a similar log on the client and the server.

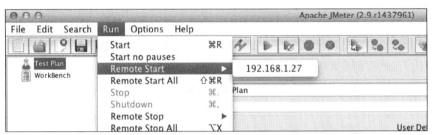

The Remote Start menu

The following will appear on the JMeter GUI client console:

```
Using remote object: UnicastRef [liveRef: [endpoint:[192.168.1.27:46313]
(remote),objID:[62a8e304:13da47c073a:-7fff, -369620866826328728]]]
```

The following will appear on the JMeter server console:

```
Starting the test on host 192.168.1.27 @ Tue Mar 20 02:42:12 UTC 2013
(1364265732881)
```

```
Finished the test on host 192.168.1.27 @ Tue Mar 20 02:42:13 UTC 2013
(1364265733154)
```

Congratulations! We are now able to control this slave node from the master. We can proceed with testing at this point, but since we are focusing on distributed testing in this chapter, it will help to have two or more nodes to control.

Repeat the steps we used earlier to spin off two more nodes: `node_two` and `node_three`. Add their assigned IP addresses to the `jmeter.properties` file of the master node, just as we did for `node_one`. At the end of it all, we should have three slave nodes we can control from the master node.

Now your JMeter GUI client should have three server IP addresses which you will find by navigating to **Run | Remote Start** and you can either kick-off an individual server node by targeting the server IP address of choice or start all the configured slave nodes at once by navigating to **Run | Remote Start All** (*Command + Shift + R* on Mac or *Ctrl + Shift + R* on Windows). When starting all the configured node servers, if everything has been properly configured, you should see logs similar to the following ones on the master console with each server node responding and acknowledging the kicking-off of the intended test plan:

```
Using remote object: UnicastRef [liveRef: [endpoint:[192.168.1.27:59212]
(remote),objID:[49a18727:13da4a8a955:-7fff, -4630561463080329291]]]

Using remote object: UnicastRef [liveRef: [endpoint:[192.168.1.149:51200]
(remote),objID:[46a1e04c:13da4a79d3d:-7fff, -5213066472819797239]]]

Using remote object: UnicastRef [liveRef: [endpoint:[192.168.1.6:51791]
(remote),objID:[-1434b37d:13da4a85f8a:-7fff, -2658534524006849789]]]
```

As you can see from the preceding logs, the master node makes connections with all three configured slave nodes, `192.168.1.6`, `192.168.1.27`, and `192.168.1.149`. With the connections verified, we can now pick a test plan to run and gather the results on the master node.

For our first test, we are going to execute a test that doesn't require input data. The provided test plan (`browse-apple-itunes.jmx`) navigates to Apple's iTunes website and browses around a bit for music, movies, apps, and so on. It does no data entry and therefore doesn't need any input data. Load that into the master node's JMeter GUI and kick it off on all the slave nodes. The script launches 150 users over 30 seconds and runs for two iterations. Since we are distributing this over three slave nodes, we will have a total of 450 users launched (150 users per node) and 15 users started per second; that is, 450/30. Following are the results our machine produced. It's a quad-core MacBook Pro with a 2.2 GHz processor and 8 GB of RAM. Your mileage may vary depending on the computing power of your machine.

Label	# Samples	Average	Median	90% Line	Min	Max	Error %	Throughput	KB/sec
Apple Home	900	1321	857	2554	518	7695	0.00%	8.6/sec	630.4
iTunes	900	1104	772	2083	542	5524	0.11%	8.6/sec	204.2
Featured	900	637	450	1321	336	5086	0.00%	8.9/sec	116.0
Songs	900	715	470	1676	329	12980	0.00%	8.0/sec	132.8
Albums	900	200	63	327	18	4607	0.00%	8.1/sec	108.5
TV Shows	900	672	436	1766	308	4895	0.00%	8.0/sec	132.1
Movies	900	214	56	317	18	12474	0.00%	8.1/sec	95.8
Movie Rentals	900	217	57	317	19	12429	0.00%	8.1/sec	102.0
Free Apps	900	267	61	428	16	12574	0.00%	8.1/sec	99.1
Paid Apps	900	322	62	832	17	4700	0.00%	8.1/sec	99.9
Music Videos	900	371	72	1014	17	12668	0.00%	8.2/sec	108.5
TOTAL	9900	549	341	1502	16	12980	0.01%	76.6/sec	1524.9

The aggregate report for Browse Apple iTunes distributed test

It should be noted that in our case we are still running all these virtual slave nodes on a single box, so the resources are still limited. That is, all the slaves are still sharing the resources of the host machine. Therefore, attempting to distribute more load than could originally be handled by the host machine can lead to degraded performance with high response times. However, nothing prevents you from running the provided Vagrant scripts on additional physical machines to simulate more load without worrying about constrained resources.

The second test is one we have seen before, in *Chapter 2, Recording Your First Test*. It's the Excilys banking application that requires an input data file. As JMeter only sends the test plans to slave nodes, we need to get the input files across to all the slave nodes in order to successfully execute the test. To do that, perform the following steps on the command line:

1. Go to the directory of the slave node.
2. Run the following commands in sequence:

   1. Log in to the machine:

      vagrant ssh

   2. Go to JMeter's `bin` directory:

      cd apache-jmeter-2.9/bin

   3. Get the `users2.txt` file from a remote location:

      wget https://raw.github.com/berinle/vagrant-data/master/ users2.txt

Repeat these steps for all three nodes. This puts the `users2.txt` file, which is needed by the test plan, in a location that can be seen by the JMeter server on the slave nodes. Now open the test plan (`excilys-bank-scenario-2.jmx`) on the master JMeter GUI client. Just as before, go to **Run | Remote Start All**. Feel free to increase the number of threads, ramp-ups, and iterations, but please be careful not to crash the server.

Configuring multiple slave nodes on a single box

JMeter allows you to configure multiple slave nodes on a single box as long as they are configured to broadcast on different RMI ports. This could come handy in cases where the machine you are using is powerful enough to handle it or you don't have access to additional physical machines. Just as in the previous section, we will be using Vagrant to configure a single virtual machine and spin off multiple JMeter slave nodes on it. For this illustration, I have prepared a Vagrant script with Puppet provisioning, similar to what we used in the last section. This starts up a VirtualBox; exposes port 1099 (the standard JMeter RMI port), 1664, and 1665; and installs three JMeter slave nodes named `jmeter-1`, `jmeter-2`, and `jmeter-3` on them respectively. These are the different ports that will be used by the different slave nodes when starting the server. To get started, perform the following steps:

1. Extract the provided Vagrant bundle (`978-1-78216-584-2_6_2_codes.zip`) into a directory of your choice. We will call it `VAGRANT_EXTRACT`.

2. From the command line, go to the `VAGRANT_EXTRACT` directory.

3. Run `vagrant up`.

4. Choose the appropriate connection to bridge. For example, if you are on a wireless connection, choose `en1: Wi-Fi` and if you are on Ethernet, choose `en0: Ethernet`.

5. Wait for VirtualBox to be fully built.

6. Run `vagrant ssh`.

7. Run `ls -l`.

At this point, you should see the three slave nodes present on the machine.

```
vagrant@precise32:~$ ls -l
total 388
drwxr-xr-x 7 vagrant vagrant   4096 Mar 27 10:57 jmeter-1
drwxr-xr-x 7 vagrant vagrant   4096 Mar 27 11:02 jmeter-2
drwxr-xr-x 7 vagrant vagrant   4096 Mar 27 11:02 jmeter-3
-rwxr-xr-x 1 vagrant vagrant   6487 Sep 14  2012 postinstall.sh
```

The only thing left now is to configure the RMI_HOST_DEF variable in JMETER_HOME/bin/jmeter-server, just as we did in the previous section to avoid the look back error that would be reported. From the VirtualBox, run the following on the command line:

```
ifconfig | grepinet
```

This will provide you the assigned IP address of the box.

Edit the jmeter-server script to add the box's IP address using the following steps:

1. Run vi jmeter-1/bin/jmeter-server.

2. Look for the line beginning with #RMI_HOST_DEF and replace it with RMI_HOST_DEF=-Djava.rmi.server.hostname=192.168.1.55 (replace 192.168.1.55 with the assigned IP address of your virtual box).

3. Save and close the file (press *Esc* and type :wq).

4. Repeat the process for the other two slave nodes (jmeter-2 and jmeter-3).

At this point, the slave nodes are ready to be kicked off and the only thing left to do is to start each of them up on our already configured RMI ports (1099, 1664, and 1665).

To start the jmeter-1 slave node in a new shell/console, perform the following steps:

1. Go to the VAGRANT_EXTRACT directory by using the following:

    ```
    cd VAGRANT_EXTRACT
    ```

2. SSH into the box by using the following:

    ```
    vagrant ssh
    ```

3. Start the JMeter server on the default port, 1099, by using the following:

    ```
    ./jmeter-1/bin/jmeter-server
    ```

To start the `jmeter-2` slave node in a new shell/console, perform the following steps:

1. Go to the VAGRANT_EXTRACT directory.

    cd VAGRANT_EXTRACT

2. SSH into the box.

    vagrant ssh

3. Start the JMeter server on port 1664.

    SERVER_POST=1664 ./jmeter-1/bin/jmeter-server

To start the `jmeter-3` slave node in a new shell/console, perform the following steps:

1. Go to the VAGRANT_EXTRACT directory.

    cd VAGRANT_EXTRACT

2. SSH into the box.

    vagrant ssh

3. Start the JMeter server on port 1665.

    SERVER_POST=1665 ./jmeter-1/bin/jmeter-server

Configuring the master node to be tested against multiple slave nodes on a single box

With the slave nodes configured, we need to configure the master node to communicate with them before we can proceed with executing our tests remotely. To do that, we have to add the slave nodes' IP addresses and ports to the master node's configuration file.

On the host machine (where the JMeter GUI client is running), perform the following steps:

1. Open JMETER_HOME/bin/jmeter.properties.

2. Look for the line beginning with `remote_hosts=127.0.0.1` and then:

   1. Change it to `remote_hosts=192.168.1.55:1099,` `192.168.1.55:1664, 192.168.1.55:1665.`

   2. `192.168.1.55` should be changed to match the assigned IP address of your virtual box.

3. Save the file (press *Esc* and type `:wq`).

4. Launch JMeter.

5. Navigate to **Run | Remote Start | Slave IP address**, where **Slave IP address** is the assigned IP address of your virtual machine.

With that done, we are ready to kick off our tests as we did in the previous section. The only difference now is that all our slave nodes are configured on one virtual host. Open up the `browse-apple-itunes.jmx` test plan in the JMeter GUI client on the master. Change the number of threads from 150 to 15. Now kick off the test remotely on all slave nodes. The test should complete after a while (be patient). If you compare the results of this run with the previous run that had slaves configured on separate virtual boxes, you will see quite an increase in the response times. The following screenshot shows the results we got from our run:

Label	# Samples	Average	Median	90% Line	Min	Max	Error %	Throughput	KB/sec
Apple Home	90	2519	1857	3170	564	16798	0.00%	41.3/min	50.4
iTunes	90	2365	1814	3899	611	9138	0.00%	43.8/min	17.5
Featured	90	1333	1083	2203	329	9340	0.00%	45.9/min	10.0
Songs	90	1948	1285	2880	320	18510	0.00%	46.7/min	13.0
Albums	90	570	473	1211	20	1674	0.00%	47.6/min	11.2
TV Shows	90	1243	1116	2120	322	3445	0.00%	47.7/min	13.5
Movies	90	600	471	1214	19	5291	0.00%	48.5/min	9.6
Movie Rentals	90	521	474	1088	22	1655	0.00%	48.9/min	9.7
Free Apps	90	696	409	1113	20	15982	0.00%	49.2/min	10.1
Paid Apps	90	604	315	1089	23	12594	0.00%	49.6/min	10.1
Music Videos	90	497	375	1126	19	1537	0.00%	50.1/min	11.1
TOTAL	990	1172	818	2268	19	18510	0.00%	7.0/sec	140.7

The aggregate report for Browse Apple iTunes distributed test 2

You can see we are seeing higher response times in the **90% Line** column for this run when compared with the previous run, even though this test is using far less users (15 compared to 150). One conclusion that can be drawn from these results is that spinning off multiple slave nodes on a machine is not always optimal and should not be your first choice. Your mileage may vary based on the capacity of the machine you use.

Leveraging the cloud for distributed testing

So far, we have seen how we can distribute load to various physical or virtual machines and by so doing achieve more load than could ever be possible with a single machine. Our setup thus far, though, has been internal to our network using a master/slave configuration. Sometimes, it helps to isolate any artificial bottlenecks occurring on the LAN and run your tests from more realistic locations external to your network. This has the added benefit of leveraging substantially larger hardware at minimal cost thanks to the various cloud offerings now at our disposal. Another area worth considering is the master/slave setup we have employed thus far. While this will work perfectly fine when few slaves are configured, as more slaves get added to the mix, the master node becomes a huge bottleneck. This shouldn't come as a surprise since I/O and network operations increase as more and more slave nodes try to feed ongoing testing results to the master. What would be most efficient and ideal is to have each slave node run its test in isolation in the non-GUI mode, save the results, and its cumulative results from all the slave nodes gathered at the end of the test. The challenge of course is kicking off all the test executions on all the nodes in harmony and gathering the results from each. That could be a little bit daunting, not to mention time-consuming. Thankfully, we can use Vagrant, our Swiss-Army-knife environmental setup tool, to get partly there. We will employ it to start server instances on **AWS** (**Amazon Web Service**), set up the Java Runtime Environment (JRE), JMeter, and upload our test scripts to the cloud virtual machines we bring up. Amazon has an excellent variety of cloud services that make it easy to run your whole company's infrastructure in the cloud, if you so choose. Read more about it at http://aws.amazon.com/.

Provided the application under test is accessible from outside your corporate network, the methods described here should suit your needs just fine.

The first step is to register for an AWS account, if you don't already have one. You can do that by going to http://aws.amazon.com/ and clicking on the **Sign up** button. Once registered, you'll need to obtain your access key, secret key, and a key pair to use for authenticating with the machines you create on AWS.

Obtaining your access key, secret key, and key pair

To obtain your access key, secret key, and key pair, perform the following steps:

1. Sign in to your AWS account at http://aws.amazon.com/.

2. In the upper right-hand corner, click on the **My Account/Console** drop-down list.

3. Select **Security Credentials**.

4. In the **Access Keys** tab under **Access Credentials Section**, perform the following steps:

   1. Click on **Create a new Access Key**.

   2. Note the **Access Key ID**.

   3. Click on **Show link** under **Secret Access Key** to reveal the secret access key.

5. Generate a key pair by following the instructions at `http://docs.aws.amazon.com/AWSEC2/latest/UserGuide/generating-a-keypair.html`.

   1. If you use the browser, it will create a key pair and automatically download the private key for you.

   2. Copy or move it to a location of your choice. We will use the name and location created here later.

6. With all that done, we are ready to start launching some instances in the cloud! See the following screenshot for details:

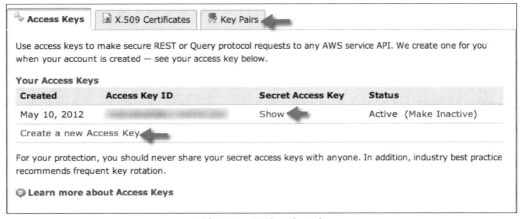

Obtaining AWS credentials

 AWS is a paid service and you are billed for every hour you have an instance up and running. At the time of writing, for a small instance that we used during the course of this section, it costs $0.10/hr for each instance, which is not bad considering all the effort it saves getting a box, setting it up, and doing it multiple times.

We have prepared a Vagrant script with Puppet provisioning, just as we did in the previous sections. The only difference this time is that is it configured to work with AWS as opposed to virtual boxes in our intranet. To use it, you need to install the Vagrant AWS plugin. Do that by running the following from the command line:

```
vagrant plugin install vagrant-aws
```

This simple one liner makes Vagrant AWS aware, and now it understands how to interact with machines on AWS. We can now transparently spin off virtual machines on Amazon's infrastructure just as we did with VirtualBox locally.

 By running the `vagrant plugin install` command, we assume you have already installed Vagrant on the machine where this operation is performed. If you haven't, please grab a copy at `http://downloads.vagrantup.com/` and proceed with the installation as directed.

Launching an AWS instance

With the Vagrant AWS plugin installed, the next step is to follow these listed instructions:

1. Download the prepared Vagrant bundle for this section (`978-1-78216-584-2_6_3_codes.zip`).

2. Extract it to a location of your choice. We will refer to this as `INSTANCE_HOME`.

3. Open the `$INSTANCE_HOME/Vagrant` file in an editor of your choice and fill in the required entries.

   ○ `aws.secret_access_key = "YOUR AWS SECRET KEY"`

   ○ `aws.keypair_name = "YOUR KEYPAIR NAME"`

   ○ `aws.ssh_private_key_path = "PATH TO YOUR PRIVATE KEY"`

   ○ `aws.region = "YOUR AWS REGION"`

   These are values as generated in the previous section, *Obtain your access key, secret key, and key pair.*

4. Save your changes.

5. From the command line, go to the directory `INSTANCE_HOME`:

   ```
   cd $INSTANCE_HOME
   ```

6. Bring up the first virtual machine on AWS.

   ```
   vagrant up vm1 --provider=aws
   ```

7. Wait for the process to complete. You will see a bunch of entries (similar to what follows) written to the console and the whole process could take up to a minute or two depending on network latency, Internet speed, communication with AWS, among others.

```
Bringing machine 'vm1' up with 'aws' provider...
[vm1] Warning! The AWS provider doesn't support any of the Vagrant
high-level network configurations (`config.vm.network`). They
will be silently ignored.
[vm1] Launching an instance with the following settings...
[vm1]   -- Type: m1.small
[vm1]   -- AMI: ami-7747d01e
[vm1]   -- Region: us-east-1
[vm1]   -- SSH Port: 22
[vm1]   -- Keypair: book-test
[vm1] Waiting for instance to become "ready"...
[vm1] Waiting for SSH to become available...
[vm1] Machine is booted and ready for use!

...

notice: /Stage[main]/Java::Package_debian/Package[java]/ensure:
ensure changed 'purged' to 'present'
notice: Finished catalog run in 113.17 seconds
```

8. Verify that you are able to connect to the box and that JMeter was successfully installed on the machine.

```
vagrant ssh vm1
```

`ls -l` This should contain a testplans directory.

`ls -l /usr/local/` This should contain some directories, including the one for JMeter:

Now our first VirtualBox is up and running, ready to execute our test plans.

Start up three additional console/shell windows, one for each additional virtual machine we will bring up. In each of the new shell windows, bring up an additional box running the following commands:

```
vagrant up vm2 --provider=aws
vagrant up vm3 --provider=aws
vagrant up vm4 --provider=aws
```

To bring up the second (vm2), third (vm3), and fourth (vm4) virtual machines respectively. Verify that each of them is properly set up, just as we did for the first virtual machine. With all four machines running, we are ready to proceed with executing our test plan.

Executing the test plan

Since we are not using a master/slave node configuration in this section for reasons described earlier, we'll need to execute the following command on all four virtual machines simultaneously as best we can.

To execute our test plan, run the following on the virtual boxes:

On **vm1**, type (or copy) the following on the console:

```
/usr/local/jmeter/bin/jmeter -n -t testplans/browse-apple-itunes.jmx -l
vm1-out.csv
```

On **vm2**, type (or copy) the following on the console:

```
/usr/local/jmeter/bin/jmeter -n -t testplans/browse-apple-itunes.jmx -l
vm2-out.csv
```

On **vm3**, type (or copy) the following on the console:

```
/usr/local/jmeter/bin/jmeter -n -t testplans/browse-apple-itunes.jmx -l
vm3-out.csv
```

On **vm4**, type (or copy) the following on the console:

```
/usr/local/jmeter/bin/jmeter -n -t testplans/browse-apple-itunes.jmx -l
vm4-out.csv
```

These will run JMeter in the non-GUI mode and execute the browse-apple-itunes. jmx test plan. Each virtual machine will print simulation results to CSV files. So **vm1** will output results to vm1-out.csv, **vm2** to vm2-out.csv, and so on.

Now that all the consoles are ready, press *Enter* on your keyboard in each console to execute the test plan on each virtual machine. You should see a log similar to the following on each console:

```
Created the tree successfully using testplans/browse-apple-itunes.jmx
Starting the test @ Thu Apr 04 20:49:38 UTC 2013 (1365108578406)
Waiting for possible shutdown message on port 4445
Generate Summary Results +   3592 in    82s =   43.9/s Avg:  1030 Min:
4 Max:  7299 Err:    0 (0.00%) Active: 208 Started: 300 Finished: 92
```

```
Generate Summary Results +    3008 in     55s =    54.8/s Avg:    541 Min:
4 Max:   6508 Err:      0 (0.00%) Active: 0 Started: 300 Finished: 300

Generate Summary Results =    6600 in    114s =    57.7/s Avg:    807 Min:
4 Max:   7299 Err:      0 (0.00%)

Tidying up ...      @ Thu Apr 04 20:51:34 UTC 2013 (1365108694177)

... end of run
```

The last line (`... end of run`) indicates the test has finished on that node and the result is ready for viewing. You should be able to verify the results file was generated by listing the contents of the current directory using the `ls -l` command. You should see an output of the format `vmX-out.csv` (where X represents the node you are on. 1, 2, 3, or 4 in our case).

Viewing the results from the virtual machines

To view the results, we need to grab the files from each host machine and then concatenate them together to form a composite whole. We can then view the final merged file using a JMeter GUI client. To grab the files, we can use any SFTP tool of our choice. If you are on a Unix-flavored machine, chances are that you already have the `scp` command-line utility handy. That is what we will be using here. To proceed, we will need the name of the host machine we are trying to connect to. To get that, type in the `exit` command on the console of the first virtual machine.

You will see lines similar to the following:

```
ubuntu@ip-10-190-237-149:~$ exit

logout

Connection to ec2-23-23-1-249.compute-1.amazonaws.com closed.
```

`ec2-xxxxxx.compute-1.amazonaws.com` is the host name of the machine. We can now connect to the box using our `keypair` file and retrieve the results file. On the console, issue the following command:

```
scp -i [PATH TO YOUR KEYPAIR FILE] ubuntu@[HOSTNAME]:"*.csv" [DESTINATION
DIRECTORY ON LOCAL MACHINE]
```

As an example, on our box, our `keypair` file named `book-test.pem` is stored under the `.ec2` directory in our home directory and we want to place the results file in `/tmp directory`. So we run the following command:

```
scp -i ~/.ec2/book-test.pem ubuntu@ec2-23-23-1-249.compute-1.amazonaws.
com:"*.csv" /tmp
```

This will transfer all the `.csv` files on the AWS instance to our local machine under the `/tmp` directory.

Repeat the command for the three additional virtual boxes.

 Remember to use the correct hostname for each of the virtual boxes.

After transferring all the result files from the virtual machines, we can terminate all the instances since we are done with them.

 AWS is a paid service and you are charged per hour per instance. If you are done with a box, remember to shut it down, else you will incur unneeded charges.

You can either shut down each individually using vagrant destroy [VM ALIAS NAME] (vagrant destroy vm1 will shut down the virtual box aliased vm1) or shut down all running instances using vagrant destroy.

 You can always verify the state of your instances through the vagrant status command or through the AWS web console, at https://console.aws.amazon.com/ec2.

With our entire results file from all hosts now available locally, we will need to merge them together to get an aggregate of response time across all hosts. We can do this with any editor that can deal with CSV file formats. Basically, you will open a file (say vm1-out.csv) and append the entire contents of the other files (vm2-out.csv, vm3-out.csv, and vm4-out.csv) into it. Alternatively, this can all be done from the command line. For those on Unix-flavored machines, the cat command can be employed. Open the command line and go to the directory where you have transferred the result files. Then run the following on the console:

```
cat vm1-out.csv vm2-out.csv vm3-out.csv vm4-out.csv >> merged-out.csv
```

 This assumes you have followed along with this section and named your result files vm1-out.csv through vm4-out.csv.

This creates a file named `merged-out.csv` that can now be opened in our JMeter GUI client. To do that, perform the following steps:

1. Launch the JMeter GUI.
2. Add a Summary Report listener by navigating to **Test Plan | Add | Listener | Summary Report**.
3. Click on **Summary Report**.
4. Click on the **Browse...** button.
5. Select the `merged-out.csv` file.

Since our test plan spins off 300 users and runs for two iterations, each virtual node generates 600 samples. Since we ran this across four nodes, we have a total of 2,400 samplers generated, as can be seen from the following screenshot. We also see that the **Max** response time is not too shabby. There were no errors reported on any of the nodes and the throughput was good for our run. These are not bad numbers considering we used small instances of AWS. We can always put more stress on the application or web servers by spinning off more nodes to run test plans or by using higher capacity machines on AWS. Although we have only used four virtual boxes for illustrative purposes here, nothing prevents you from scaling out to hundreds of machines to run your test plan.

As you start to scale out to more and more servers for your test plans, it may become increasingly difficult and cumbersome to simultaneously start your test plans across all nodes. At the time of writing, we discovered yet another tool that promises to ease the management pain across multiple AWS nodes or in-house networked machines. The tool helps spin off AWS instances (as we have done here); install JMeter; run a test plan, distributing the load across the number of instances spun; and gathers all the results from all hosts to your local box, all the while giving you real time aggregate information on the console.

At the end of the tests, it terminates all AWS instances that were started. We gave it a spin, but couldn't quite get it working as advertised. It is still worth keeping an eye on the project and you can find out more about it at `https://github.com/oliverlloyd/jmeter-ec2`. Furthermore, we should mention that there are some services out on the Web helping to bring ease to distributed testing. Two such services are Gridinit (`http://gridinit.com/`) and BlazeMeter (`http://blazemeter.com/`). They are both worth checking out.

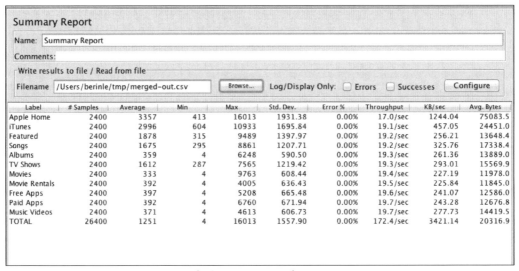

Label	# Samples	Average	Min	Max	Std. Dev.	Error %	Throughput	KB/sec	Avg. Bytes
Apple Home	2400	3357	413	16013	1931.38	0.00%	17.0/sec	1244.04	75083.5
iTunes	2400	2996	604	10933	1695.84	0.00%	19.1/sec	457.05	24451.0
Featured	2400	1878	315	9489	1397.97	0.00%	19.2/sec	256.21	13648.4
Songs	2400	1675	295	8861	1207.71	0.00%	19.2/sec	325.76	17338.4
Albums	2400	359	4	6248	590.50	0.00%	19.3/sec	261.36	13889.0
TV Shows	2400	1612	287	7565	1219.42	0.00%	19.3/sec	293.01	15569.9
Movies	2400	333	4	9763	608.44	0.00%	19.4/sec	227.19	11978.0
Movie Rentals	2400	392	4	4005	636.43	0.00%	19.5/sec	225.84	11845.0
Free Apps	2400	397	4	5208	665.48	0.00%	19.6/sec	241.07	12586.0
Paid Apps	2400	392	4	6760	671.94	0.00%	19.7/sec	243.28	12676.8
Music Videos	2400	371	4	4613	606.73	0.00%	19.7/sec	277.73	14419.5
TOTAL	26400	1251	4	16013	1557.90	0.00%	172.4/sec	3421.14	20316.9

The Summary Report listener

With that, we wrap up our look into distributed testing with JMeter. Though the test plan we used had no input test data, nothing prevents you from using one that does. Also, all the other techniques we have learned in other chapters can be applied whenever they make sense. Also, not using a master/node configuration got us past the hurdle of known limitations. These include:

- Network saturation due to high number of slave nodes writing to the master node

- RMI communication is not possible across subnets without a proxy, thereby forcing slaves and the master to be on the same subnet

- The master node server could be easily overwhelmed with very few slave nodes reporting to it, depending on its resources (CPU and memory)

Summary

We have covered quite a lot of ground in this chapter. We have learned how we can distribute load using different techniques when executing test plans. We learned how to have JMeter work in a master/node configuration. With the help of tools such as Vagrant and Puppet, we made a daunting task really easy. We learned how to spin off several node machines on the same physical box (or different boxes) and use a master node to control them all from a JMeter GUI. While convenient, we saw that this method was limiting in terms of scalability. As the number of slave nodes grew, the master quickly became the bottleneck due to high I/O generated from several nodes trying to report progress to it. To overcome such restrictions and ultimately achieve infinite scalability, we learned how to run several test machines in parallel to execute our test plans. In the process, we leveraged the AWS infrastructure and saw how we can use the cloud to aid testing more efficiently, thus helping us reach our targeted goals.

In the next chapter, we will look at some tips that are helpful to have handy when working with JMeter.

7
Helpful Tips

At this point, you have hopefully become familiar with the inner workings of JMeter and are comfortable with using it to achieve most of your testing needs. However, before we wrap up the book, there are some helpful tips worth mentioning that will make working with JMeter more pleasant and perhaps save you time in the process. These are some techniques we have learned over the years and they have proven useful in almost every environment we have found ourselves.

JMeter properties and variables

JMeter properties are defined in `jmeter.properties`, which is global in nature and used to define some defaults that JMeter uses. The value of the `remote_hosts` property encountered in the previous chapter is a good example of this. Properties can be referenced from within a test plan, but cannot be used for thread-specific values because of their global nature (shared among all threads).

JMeter variables, on the other hand, are local to each thread. The values may stay the same or vary between threads. In cases where a variable is updated by a thread, only the thread copy of the variable is changed, thus remaining invisible to other running threads. A good example of this is the Regular Expression Extractor post processor we encountered in the previous chapters. The values extracted and acted upon are in the context of the samples of the running thread. The variables that are extracted are user-defined and available to the whole test plan at startup. If the same variable is defined by multiple user-defined variable elements, the last one wins.

As simple as they appear, using JMeter variables wisely can save you time by allowing you to use the same recorded scripts from one environment to another environment without having to rescript for every single environment you are targeting, provided the two environments are structured similarly architecturally. So, for instance, test plans recorded against the **User Acceptance Test (UAT)** environment can be run in production if those two environments bear a resemblance in structure. To accomplish that, you can either define User Defined Variables (UDV) at the Test Plan root level, or replace individual URLs for HTTP Request samplers. For example, we can define the following UDVs at the Test plan root level:

Name	Value
app_url	${__P(app_url, https://uat.fastcompany.com/someapp)}
sso_url	${__P(sso_url, https://sso.uat.fastcompany.com/login)}
threads	${__P(threads, 10)}
loops	${__P(loops, 30)}

With such a configuration, we have defined default values for app_url, sso_url, threads, and loops and still provided the ability to override them from the command line as follows:

```
jmeter ... -Japp_url=https://fastcompany.com/someapp Jsso_url=https://
sso.fastcompany.com/login -Jloops=15
```

This will make our test plans use an app_url variable having the value https://fastcompany.com/someapp, an sso_url variable having the value https://sso.fastcompany.com/login, and the loops variable having the value 15. The number of threads will remain 10 (the default) since it wasn't overridden. This concept saves a lot of time when developing test plans against various environments, allowing you to record once and target various environments with the same set of scripts. For instance, this is useful when a particular environment isn't ready yet and scripts have already been developed targeting an active environment. Once the environment becomes available, the same scripts can target the newly available environment without having to rerecord them.

We have bundled a sample with the book (`excilys-bank-scenario-3.jmx`). It's from the banking application sample test plan we saw in , *Recording Your First Test*. It is hosted on two different cloud providers: Cloudbees at `http://excilysbank.gatling.cloudbees.net` and AppFog at `http://excilysbank.aws.af.cm`. It runs against AppFog by default. To run it against Cloudbees, you will need to override the hostname variable when you start JMeter like so:

```
jmeter -Jhostname=excilysbank.gatling.cloudbees.net
```

JMeter functions

JMeter functions are special values that can populate fields or any sampler or other element in the test plan. They take the following form:

```
${__functionName(var1,var2,var3)}
```

Here, `__functionName` matches any of the many function names JMeter offers. Parentheses surround the parameters sent to the function, which can vary from function to function. Functions with no parameters don't need the parentheses; for example, `${__threadNum}`. A list of all the available functions can be found on JMeter's website at `http://jmeter.apache.org/usermanual/functions.html`. Functions are divided into seven main categories. They are given here along with their examples:

- **Information**: `threadNum` `machineIP`, `time`, and so on
- **Input** : `CSVRead`, `XPath`, and so on
- **Calculation**: `counter`, `random`, `UUID`, and so on
- **Scripting**: `javaScript`, `BeanShell`, and so on
- **Properties**: `property`, `P`, `setProperty`, and so on
- **Variables**: `split`, `eval`, and so on
- **String**: `char`, `unescape`, and so on

Functions can prove useful in certain situations, allowing the computation of new values at runtime based on previous response data, which thread the function is in, time, and numerous other sources. Their values are generated afresh for every request throughout the course of the test. There are also some restrictions regarding where certain functions can be invoked. Since JMeter thread variables are not fully initialized when functions are processed, variable names passed as parameters will not be set up, causing variable references to fail.

 Functions are shared between threads in the test plan. Each occurrence of a function call is handled by a separate function instance.

The Regular Expression tester

Throughout the course of the book, we have seen Regular Expression Extractor post processors in action in several of our scenarios. These components allow you to extract values from a server response using a Perl-type regular expression. As a post processor, this element executes after each sample request in its scope, applying the regular expression; extracts the requested values, generating the template string; and finally stores the result into a given variable name, which can then be referenced further down the test plan.

To fully maximize the use of the Regular Expression Extractor post processor, it helps to get acquainted with regular expressions in general. There are numerous online resources that can help, but you can start with this one: http://www.regular-expressions.info/tutorial.html. The **RegExp Tester** view is one of the options you can choose from the View Results Tree listener dropdown menu items. It allows you to test various regular expressions against the server response on a per-sampler basis. When you are interested in extracting a variable or group of variables that vary dynamically based on which thread is currently executing, this gives you the maximum flexibility to test and tune your regular expression until you find the exact match that suits your needs. Without such an element, significant time could be spent nailing down the right pattern matcher, as it would involve rerunning your test plan several times with various inaccurate expressions, hoping it eventually matches.

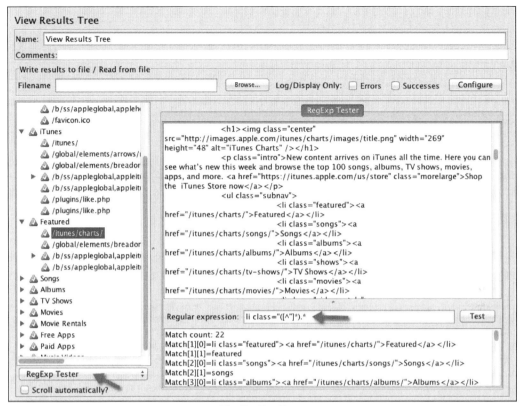

The RegExp Tester

In our browse iTunes store test plan from the previous chapter, say we were interested in extracting the `class` elements from the HTML response of the /itunes/charts/ sampler. Once the test has been exercised, we could explore the **RegExp Tester** view to find the right regular expression for this. For our purpose, it came down to `li class="([^"]*).*`, which matched 22 elements, listed in the bottom half of the window as seen in the previous screenshot. We can then copy that pattern into a Regular Expression Extractor post processor under the /itunes/charts/ sampler and store the results in a variable to use further down the chain in our test plan.

The Debug sampler

The debug sampler generates a sample containing all the values of JMeter variables and/or properties. A View Results Tree listener must be present in the test plan to view its results. This nifty component helps you debug your test plans appropriately, providing you with the tools to analyze the runtime-assigned values of various variables during test execution. In our example above, suppose we added a **Regular Expression Extractor** post processor to the /itunes/charts sampler and stored it in a variable. We can view the value assigned to the variable, and more importantly how to get to the different values if there is more than one match. To add a **Debug** sampler, right-click on **Thread Group** and navigate to **Add | Sampler | Debug Sampler**.

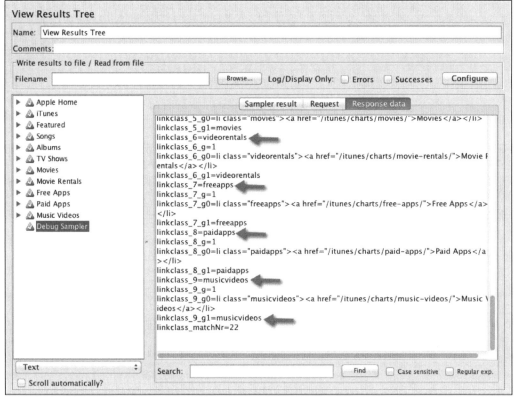

The Debug sampler via the View Result listener

As you can see from this screenshot, the multiple matches are stored under linkclass_n (where n is a match position), followed by the variable name declared in our Regular Expression Extractor post processor. Thus we can get hold of the first match as linkclass_1, the second as linkclass_2, and so on As you record more and more complex scripts, you will find the debug sampler to be an invaluable component that is worth keeping handy.

Using timers in your test plan

By default, JMeter doesn't put timers in your test plans when a scenario is recorded. This is far from reality. Ideally, users will have a think or wait time between page views and requests. Getting JMeter to simulate such pauses or waits makes your test plans more realistic, bringing it closer to how actual users might behave. JMeter offers various built-in timer components that help achieve this. Each varies from the others in how it varies the simulated pauses. The following is a list of included timers as of the time of writing.

The Constant timer

The Constant timer is used if you want each thread to pause for the same amount of time between requests.

The Gaussian random timer

The Gaussian random timer pauses each thread request for a random amount of time with most of the time intervals occurring near a particular value. The total delay is the sum of the Gaussian distributed value times, the value specified, and the offset.

The Uniform random timer

The Uniform random timer pauses thread requests for a random amount of time, with each time interval having the same probability of occurring. The total delay is the sum of the random and offset values.

The Constant throughput timer

The Constant throughput timer introduces variable pauses calculated to keep the total throughput that is, samples per minute as close as possible to the targeted figure. Though called a constant throughput timer, the throughput can be varied by using a counter value, JavaScript value, BeanShell value, or remote BeanShell server.

The Synchronizing timer

The Synchronizing timer helps simulate large instantaneous loads on various points in the test plan by blocking threads until a certain number of threads have been blocked, then releasing them all at once.

The Poisson random timer

The Poisson random timer, like the Gaussian random timer, pauses thread requests for a random amount of time, with most of the time intervals occurring near a particular value. The total delay is the sum of the Poisson distributed value and the offset value.

Any of these timers can be added by right-clicking on a **Thread Group** and navigating to **Add | Timer | (Timer to Add)**. You can read more about each of these and more at JMeter's website at `http://jmeter.apache.org/usermanual/component_reference.html#timers`.

The JDBC Request sampler

Sometimes, it's necessary to test durability and I/O operations against the database directly. How fast are inserts, updates, and selects on the tables in question? For such tests, JMeter provides a JDBC Request sampler to help issue SQL queries against the database. However, to use it, we need to set up a JDBC Connection Configuration component. Setting up this component requires us to point to a database. So let's go ahead and set up the database. Normally, this will already be set up for you to test against, but for illustrative purposes, we are going to assume none has been set up. We will be using H2, an open source pure Java SQL database. It is lightweight and relatively easy to set up.

Setting up an H2 database

1. Download a distribution at `http://www.h2database.com/html/download.html`.

2. Extract the archive to a location of your choosing. We will refer to this as `H2_HOME`.

3. From the command line, go to the `H2_HOME/bin` folder.

4. Start the H2 database server by issuing either of these commands.

    ◦ On Unix:

      `./h2.sh`

    ◦ On Windows:

      `h2.bat`

5. This will launch your browser and point to the H2 Admin console as seen in the following screenshot.

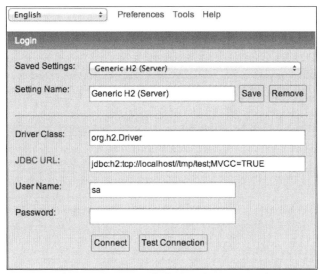

The H2 Admin console (before the connection)

6. Create a test database named `test` by changing your **JDBC URL** value to either of the following:

   ○ On Unix:

   jdbc:h2:tcp://localhost//tmp/test;MVCC=TRUE

   ○ On Windows:

   jdbc:h2:tcp://localhost/c:/test;MVCC=TRUE

7. Click on the **Connect** button.

8. Create the sample table we will be using to test by copying the following script into the space provided in the console (see the following screenshot).

```
DROP TABLE IF EXISTS TEST;
CREATE TABLE TEST(ID INT PRIMARY KEY, NAME VARCHAR(255));
INSERT INTO TEST VALUES(1, 'Hello');
INSERT INTO TEST VALUES(2, 'World');
```

9. Click on the **Run** button.

Now that we have a database and table to test with, we can go ahead and configure a **JDBC Connection Configuration** component to point to it.

Since H2 is Java-based, to run it, you need to have a JRE (Java Runtime Environment) set up on the machine of choice. Please refer to *Chapter 1, Performance Testing Fundamentals,* for instructions on setting up JRE on your machine if you don't already have it.

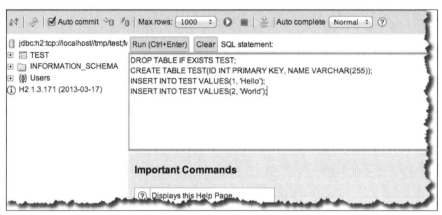

The H2 Admin console (after the connection)

Configuring a JDBC Connection Configuration component

As the name suggests, this component helps create a connection to the database from the supplied settings. Each thread could get its own dedicated connection, or connections may be pooled between threads.

1. Copy the JDBC driver (`h2-1.3.171.jar` or similar) from the `H2_HOME/bin` folder to the `JMETER_HOME/lib/ext` folder.

2. Add a JDBC Connection Configuration component to the test plan by right-clicking on **Test Plan** and navigating to **Test Plan | Add | Config Element | JDBC Connection Configuration**

3. Configure the properties as follows:

   ◦ **Variable Name**: `testPool`

   ◦ **Validation Query**: `Select 1 from dual`

   ◦ **Database URL**: `jdbc:h2:tcp://localhost//tmp/test;MVCC=TRUE` (those using Windows should use `jdbc:h2:tcp://localhost/c:/test;MVCC=TRUE`)

   ◦ **JDBC Driver class**: `org.h2.Driver`

   ◦ **Username**: `sa`

4. Leave the rest of the configuration as is.

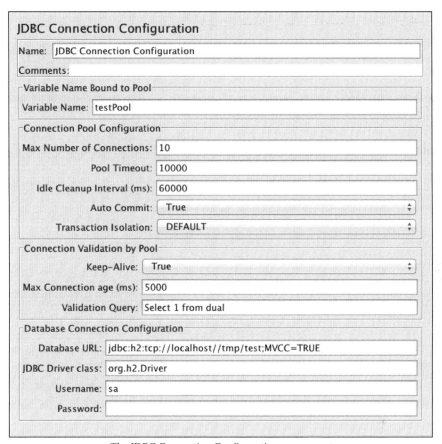

The JDBC Connection Configuration component

Adding a JDBC Request sampler

Now that we have a **JDBC Connection Configuration** component configured, the final step is to add a **JDBC Request** sampler to our test plan to make use of it. Adding that is no different from how we have added other samplers throughout the book.

1. Create a Thread Group element, if none already exist, by right-clicking on **Test Plan** and navigating to **Test Plan** | **Threads** | **Thread Group**.

2. Add a JDBC Request sampler by right-clicking on **Thread Group** and navigating to **Thread Group** | **Add** | **Sampler** | **JDBC Request**.

3. In the SQL Query input field, type in the following:

```
SELECT * FROM TEST
```

4. Add a View Results Tree listener by right-clicking on **Thread Group** and navigating to **Add | Listener | View Results Tree**.

5. Save the test plan.

6. Execute the test.

Although a simple query, it illustrates the concept. The **JDBC Request** sampler allows you to issue complex queries with bind parameters, inserts, updates, deletes, and even stored procedures. More details can be found at `http://jmeter.apache.org/usermanual/build-db-test-plan.html` and `http://jmeter.apache.org/usermanual/component_reference.html#JDBC_Request`.

A Dummy sampler

Though not part of the built-in JMeter samplers, this sampler can be added to your JMeter toolkit via the JMeter extensions project. We discussed this in detail in *Chapter 5, Resource Monitoring*, so if you don't already have it configured, please refer to that chapter to get the gist of it. This sampler generates samples with just the values that are defined for it. It comes in extremely handy when debugging post processors without having to repeat the entire execution of the test plan or waiting for the exact condition in the application under testing.

This component allows you to determine if the response should be marked a successful sample, what response code to return, the response message, the latency, and response times. In addition, it allows you to specify a request and a response, which can be anything you choose; for example, HTML, XML, and JSON.

Once the plugins have been properly installed into your JMeter instance, you should see additional samplers available to pick from.

1. Add a Thread Group element to the **Test Plan** by right-clicking on **Test Plan** and navigating to **Threads | Thread Group**.

2. Add a Dummy Sampler element by right-clicking on **Thread Group** and navigating to **Add | Sampler | jp@gc - Dummy Sampler**. For the contents of the Response Data, add the following HTML snippet:

```html
<html>
<head>
  <title>Welcome to Debug Sampler</title>
</head>
<body>
  This is a test
</body>
</html>
```

3. Add a View Results Tree listener by right-clicking on **Thread Group** and navigating to **Add | Listener | View Results Tree**.

4. Save the test plan.

5. Execute the test.

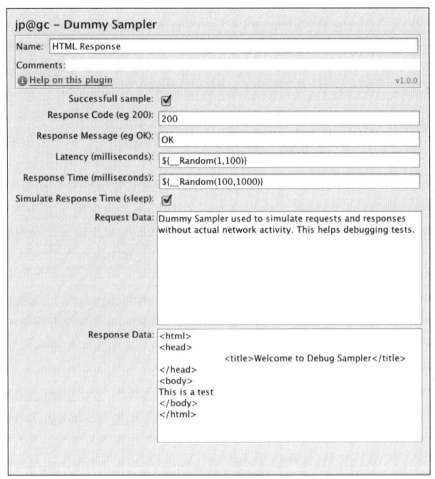

The Dummy Sampler

See the bundled `dummy-sampler.jmx` file for the full example.

The JSON Path Extractor element

Another helpful nugget in the JMeter plugin's project is the JSON Path Extractor element. This makes working with JSON pure bliss. It helps extract data out of a JSON response using JSONPath syntax (`http://goessner.net/articles/ JsonPath/index.html#e2`). For complex JSON structures, using JMeter's bundled XPath Extractor can sometimes lead to heartache when trying to get at targeted elements. Where XPath Extractor fails, JSON Path Extractor shines.

Consider a JSON structure like the following:

```
{ "store": {
    "book": [
{ "category": "reference",
        "author": "Nigel Rees",
        "title": "Sayings of the Century",
        "price": 8.95
      },
{ "category": "fiction",
        "author": "Evelyn Waugh",
        "title": "Sword of Honour",
        "price": 12.99
      },
{ "category": "fiction",
        "author": "Herman Melville",
        "title": "Moby Dick",
        "isbn": "0-553-21311-3",
        "price": 8.99
      },
{ "category": "fiction",
        "author": "J. R. R. Tolkien",
        "title": "The Lord of the Rings",
        "isbn": "0-395-19395-8",
        "price": 22.99
      }
    ],
    "bicycle": {
      "color": "red",
      "price": 19.95
    }
  }
}
```

If you wanted to get to the title of the second book in the store, an expression such as `$.store.book[1].title` gets you there swiftly. No matter how nested the structure is, JSON Path Extractor gets the job done elegantly. See the two examples that accomplish this in the book: `JSONPathExtractorExample.jmx` (from the JMeter plugin's site) and `dummy-sampler.jmx`.

Handling RESTful web services

An increasing number of applications are shifting to RESTful web services due to their simplicity to build, test, and consume compared to their SOAP counterparts. All REST communication is done over the HTTP protocol between the parties involved. HTTP is used for CRUD (create, read, update, and delete) operations. The built-in **HTTP Request** sampler in JMeter is more than up to the task. It supports GET, POST, PUT, and DELETE operations, among other things. The body of the request can be in XML or JSON format. An HTTP Header Manager component can be used to send additional HTTP header attributes if needed.

In our sample, we are going to create a new person in our sample application using a POST request, and then verify that the person was actually created using a GET request.

1. Create a new test plan.

2. Add a new Thread Group (by navigating to **Test Plan** | **Add** | **Thread Group**).

3. Add an HTTP Request sampler (this retrieves all the people records in our application so far), by navigating to **Thread Group** | **Add** | **Sampler** | **HTTP Request**. Call it `Get All People`. You will get the following fields. Fill in their values as given here:
    - **Server Name**: `jmeterbook.aws.af.cm`
    - **Method**: GET
    - **Path**: `/person/list`

4. Add another HTTP Request sampler by navigating to **Thread Group** | **Add** | **Sampler** | **HTTP Request** (this will create a new person record). Call it `Save Person()`.
    - **Server Name**: `jmeterbook.aws.af.cm`
    - **Method**: POST
    - **Post Body**: `{"firstName":"Test", "lastName":"Jmeter", "jobs":[{"id":5}]}`

5. Add a JSON Path Extractor element as a child element of the `Save Person` sampler.
   ○ **Name**: `person_id`
   ○ **JSON path**: `$.id`

6. Add another HTTP Request sampler (this will retrieve the newly created person using the extracted ID). Call it `Get Person`.
   ○ **Server Name**: `jmeterbook.aws.af.cm`
   ○ **Method**: `GET`
   ○ **Path**: `/person/get/${person_id}`

7. Add a View Results Tree listener.

8. Save the test plan.

9. Execute the test plan.

If all was correctly done, a new person with the name **Test JMeter** will be created in our application and you can verify this by pointing your browser to `http://jmeterbook.aws.af.cm/person/list`. By the same token, we can issue `DELETE` and `PUT` requests to delete and update resources if our application supports it.

Summary

In this chapter, we have learned some helpful tips that are essential to making testing with JMeter more efficient. We have covered variables, functions, regular expression testers, and timers, to name a few. Along the way, we covered some additional helpful components provided by the excellent JMeter plugin extensions. We barely scratched the surface of the additional components it provides. We looked at JSON Path Extractor and Dummy Sampler to name a few. For a full list of all components, we will encourage you to read up on their website at `https://code.google.com/p/jmeter-plugins/`. Finally, we looked at how JMeter can help us work with the database and REST web services.

We hope by now you know enough about JMeter to become proficient and attain your testing goals. In just a short time, you have grown from novice to pro. Though we couldn't cover all JMeter has to offer, we hope we have covered enough to make you see it as a valuable tool of choice when embarking on your next performance testing engagement and that you have enjoyed reading the book as much as we have had writing it.

Index

S

sampler controllers 46
samplers
  about 47
  FTP Request 47
  HTTP Request 47
  JDBC Request 47
  LDAP Request 47
  Soap/XML-RPC request 47
  Web service (SOAP) request 47
search_paths, command-line options 25
server
  monitoring, with JMeter plugin 84
session management
  with cookies 66-69
  with URL rewriting 70-73
shutdown.sh script 19
simple forms
  BSF PostProcessor 60, 62
  capturing 51
  checkboxes, handling 52
  file downloads, handling 54
  file uploads, handling 53, 54
  JSON data, posting 55-58
  JSON data, reading 59, 60
  radio buttons, handling 53
  XML response, handling 62-64
stoptest.sh script 19
stress testing 14
Synchronizing timer 121
system.properties, command-line options 25

T

test fragments 48
testing tools 15
Test Plan 45, 46
Thread Groups 46
timers
  about 48
  Constant throughput timer 121
  Constant timer 121
  Gaussian random timer 121
  Poisson random timer 122
  Synchronizing timer 121
  Uniform random timer 121
  using 121
Tomcat users
  configuring 80
Transactions per Second listener
  adding 86

U

Uniform random timer 121
URL rewriting
  about 70
  used, for managing sessions 70-73
user.classpath, command-line options 25
user.properties, command-line options 25

X

XML (Extensible Markup Language) 62
xml.parser, command-line options 24
XML response, simple forms
  handling 62-64

Thank you for buying
Performance Testing with JMeter 2.9

About Packt Publishing

Packt, pronounced 'packed', published its first book *"Mastering phpMyAdmin for Effective MySQL Management"* in April 2004 and subsequently continued to specialize in publishing highly focused books on specific technologies and solutions.

Our books and publications share the experiences of your fellow IT professionals in adapting and customizing today's systems, applications, and frameworks. Our solution based books give you the knowledge and power to customize the software and technologies you're using to get the job done. Packt books are more specific and less general than the IT books you have seen in the past. Our unique business model allows us to bring you more focused information, giving you more of what you need to know, and less of what you don't.

Packt is a modern, yet unique publishing company, which focuses on producing quality, cutting-edge books for communities of developers, administrators, and newbies alike. For more information, please visit our website: www.packtpub.com.

About Packt Open Source

In 2010, Packt launched two new brands, Packt Open Source and Packt Enterprise, in order to continue its focus on specialization. This book is part of the Packt Open Source brand, home to books published on software built around Open Source licenses, and offering information to anybody from advanced developers to budding web designers. The Open Source brand also runs Packt's Open Source Royalty Scheme, by which Packt gives a royalty to each Open Source project about whose software a book is sold.

Writing for Packt

We welcome all inquiries from people who are interested in authoring. Book proposals should be sent to author@packtpub.com. If your book idea is still at an early stage and you would like to discuss it first before writing a formal book proposal, contact us; one of our commissioning editors will get in touch with you.

We're not just looking for published authors; if you have strong technical skills but no writing experience, our experienced editors can help you develop a writing career, or simply get some additional reward for your expertise.

Learning jQuery, Third Edition

ISBN: 978-1-84951-654-9   Paperback: 428 pages

Create better interaction, design, and web development with simple JavaScript techniques

1. An introduction to jQuery that requires minimal programming experience

2. Detailed solutions to specific client-side problems

3. Revised and updated version of this popular jQuery book

Getting Started with Oracle Data Integrator 11*g*: A Hands-On Tutorial

ISBN: 978-1-84968-068-4   Paperback: 384 pages

Combine high volume data movement, complex transformations and real-time data integration with the robust capabilities of ODI in this practical guide

1. Discover the comprehensive and sophisticated orchestration of data integration tasks made possible with ODI, including monitoring and error-management

2. Get to grips with the product architecture and building data integration processes with technologies including Oracle, Microsoft SQL Server and XML files

Please check **www.PacktPub.com** for information on our titles

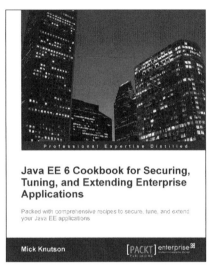

Java EE 6 Cookbook for Securing, Tuning, and Extending Enterprise Applications

ISBN: 978-1-84968-316-6   Paperback: 356 pages

Packed with comprehensive recipes to secure, tune, and extend your Java EE applications

1. Secure your Java applications using Java EE built-in features as well as the well-known Spring Security framework

2. Utilize related recipes for testing various Java EE technologies including JPA, EJB, JSF, and Web services

3. Explore various ways to extend a Java EE environment with the use of additional dynamic languages as well as frameworks

JBoss ESB Beginner's Guide

ISBN: 978-1-84951-658-7   Paperback: 320 pages

A comprehensive, practical guide to developing service-based applications using the Open Source JBoss Enterprise Service Bus

1. Develop your own service-based applications, from simple deployments through to complex legacy integrations.

2. Learn how services can communicate with each other and the benefits to be gained from loose coupling.

3. Contains clear, practical instructions for service development, highlighted through the use of numerous working examples.

Please check **www.PacktPub.com** for information on our titles

Printed in Great Britain
by Amazon.co.uk, Ltd.,
Marston Gate.